Rainwater Management in Rainfed Areas

The Authors

Dr. D.H. Ranade graduated in Agricultural Engineering from JNKVV, Jabalpur, post graduate in Soil and Water Conservation Engineering from I.I.T. Kharagpur and doctorate in Civil Engineering from DAVV, Indore. He has more than three decades of experience in research and extension of natural resource management aspects particularly in rainfed agricultural system. He is a recipient of ICAR, New Delhi's prestigious "Dr. Vasantrao Naik award 2009" for his outstanding research in the field of rainwater and dryland agriculture. At present, he is looking after the research activities in All India Coordinated Research Project on Dryland Agriculture, College of Agriculture, RVSKVV campus Indore as Chief Scientist.

Er. M.L. Jadav graduated in Agricultural Engineering from JNKVV, Jabalpur, postgraduate in Soil and Water Conservation Engineering from I.I.T. Kharagpur. He is a recipient of GATE fellowship by the University Grants Commission. He has more than twelve years of experience in teaching, research and extension in natural resource management aspects particularly in rainfed agricultural system. At present, he is looking after the research activities in All India Coordinated Research Project on Dryland Agriculture, College of Agriculture, RVSKVV campus Indore as a Scientist.

Dr. Indu Swarup graduated in Bio-Science from Rani Durgawati University, Jabalpur, post graduate in Plant Breeding and Genetics from JNKVV, Jabalpur and doctorate in Genetics from Barkatulla University, Bhopal. She has more than three decades of experience in research, extension and teaching of Plant Breeding and Genetics aspects particularly in rainfed agricultural system. At present, she is looking after the research activities in All India Coordinated Research Project on Chickpea, College of Agriculture, RVSKVV campus Indore as Principal Scientist.

Dr. O.P. Girothia graduated in B.Sc. Agriculture and Post Graduate in Agronomy from J.N.K.V.V. Jabalpur (MP) and doctorate in Agronomy from Mahatma Gandhi Chitrakoot Gramoday Vishwavidyalaya, Satna (MP). He has more than three decades of experience in research and extension of resource management aspects particularly in *rainfed* agricultural system. He has received *"Bharat Shiksha Ratan"* award on 7th April, 2018, from Global Society for Health and Educational Growth, New Delhi. At present, he is looking after the research activities in all Indian Coordinated Research Project on Dryland Agriculture, College of Agriculture, R.V.S.K.V.V. campus, Indore (MP) as Senior Technical Officer (T6).

Dr. D.V. Bhagat graduated in B.Sc. Agriculture and Post Graduate in Agronomy from J.N.K.V.V., Jabalpur (MP) and doctorate in Life Science (Botany) from A.P.S.V.V., Rewa (MP). He has more than three decades of experience in research and extension of resource management aspects. He has received *"Bharat Shiksha Ratan"* award on 7th April, 2018, from Global Society for Health and Educational Growth, New Delhi. At present, he is looking after the research activities in All Indian Coordinated Research Project on Dryland Agriculture, College of Agriculture, R.V.S.K.V.V. campus, Indore as Senior scientist.

Dr. Akhilesh Singh did B.Tech in Agricultural Engineering in 1999 from Allahabad Agricultural Institute, Allahabad. He completed M.Tech. and Ph.D. in Soil and Water Engineering in 2002 and 2009, respectively from JNKVV, Jabalpur. He worked as SRF and RA for more than 7 years at College of Agricultural Engineering, JNKVV, Jabalpur. Presently he is working as Scientist (Agril. Engg.) at RVSKVV, Gwalior from 201. He has published more than 15 research papers in NAAS rated journal, 12 Technical bulletins/manuals/practical manuals, one ISBN edited book.

Dr. S.K. Choudhary graduated in Agriculture, postgraduate and doctorate in Agronomy from JNKVV, Jabalpur. He has more than three decades of experience in research and extension of Seed production, Farm management, Cropping system, natural resource management aspects particularly in Farming system. At present, he is looking after the research activities in All India Coordinated Research Project on Integrated Farming System, College of Agriculture, RVSKVV campus Indore as Principal Scientist.

Rainwater Management in Rainfed Areas

– Authors –

D.H. Ranade

M.L. Jadav

Indus Swarup

O.P. Girothia

D.V. Bhagat

Akhilesh Singh

Sharad Choudhary

BIOTECH

2020

BIOTECH BOOKS®

ISBN 978-81-7622-458-1

Published by: **BIOTECH BOOKS®**
4762-63/23, Ansari Road, Darya Ganj,
New Delhi - 110 002
Phone: +91-011-43003222, 09899295259
E-mail: biotechbooks@yahoo.co.in

Typeset at: **Classic Computer Services**
Delhi - 110 035

Printed at: **Replika Press Pvt. Ltd.**

PRINTED IN INDIA

Preface

All India Coordinated Research Project for Dryland Agriculture and Operational Research Project is in operation at College of Agriculture, Indore to tackle the problems of rainfed farming by and large in demonstrational mode with emphasis on improving crop productivity of rainfed vertisols areas. It has been experienced in the research farm of the project and on these watersheds adopted under Operational Research Project for Dryland Agriculture that conservation of natural resources has been the priority of the areas. Unless these resources are made available in these watersheds, the adoption of dryland technologies generated at research farms will not be successful. Thus under the project, priority has been given more on developmental activities supplemented by other components on rainfed activities. Thus the focus of this centre is aimed at addressing natural resource management issues particularly rainwater management for rainfed agriculture. Many useful information on this important aspect have been generated while working at the station and with the farmers of rainfed vertisol of Malwa and Nimar region. These field experiences gathered from these, is now being published in form of a book entitled "Rainwater Management for rainfed areas". We hope that this book will be helpful for the academicians, policy makers, field extension workers, scientists and those working particularly in the farmers' fields for solving the problems of rainfed farming.

D.H. Ranade

M.L. Jadav

Indus Swarup

O.P. Girothia

D.V. Bhagat

Akhilesh Singh

Sharad Choudhary

Contents

Chapter 1

Enhancing Crop Productivity through Water Harvesting Tank under Changing Climatic Conditions

It is predicted that change in climate will affect soil moisture, groundwater and frequency of flood or drought at the source, finally groundwater in area. Constructions of rainwater harvesting structures have been the strategy to stop migration of the people.Thus in order to meet the increased irrigation water, augmentation of existing water sources by development of additional sources of water and conjunctive use of surface and groundwater will be needed. Rainwater harvesting technologies are among which has long beenrecognizedasa critical factor for productivity of agricultural crops. Rainwater harvesting measures could play a key role in furthermitigationstrategiesagainsttheglobal warming instead of carbon dioxide avoidance policy. Therefore, to evolve the mitigation strategy, a study was initiated during 2011 in Malwa region under NICRA (National Innovations on Climate Resilient Agriculture) Project with an objective in view to minimize the risk due to changing climatic conditions associated with farming and enable farmers to crop with these risks. As the runoff potential of black soils of Malwa region is very high due to its inherent properties, it is decided to harvest the runoff at suitable locations and its subsequent utilization with conjunctive use of groundwater. The increased water availability will thus ensure the provision of life saving and supplemental irrigation under changing climatic conditions.

The team of scientists of All India Coordinated Research Project for Dryland Agriculture, College of Agriculture, Indore have been visiting different villages of Malwa region from time to time to study about the adopted agricultural practices by the farmers. The main objective of this study is to evaluate these techniques scientifically for modifying it and to provide to the farmers for enhancing their crop production and farm income. This on-site and on-farm study also decides future research work. It has been observed by the team that for adopting scientific methods the farmers also consider various hypothesis. However, the team continuously motivating the framers to adopt these advanced practices. A similar attempt has been made by the team during 2010-11 in the village Ningnoti (22° 47'23.9N, 75° 54'17.1.9E) of Sanwer block of Indore district under project NICRA financed by ICAR, New Delhi. The main objective of this project is to reduce the adverse effect of changing climate on the crop production. For this, attempts have been made to reduce the cost of cultivation by contingent plan, enhancing irrigation water availability and use of improved farm implements.

In an initial study, it was observed in 2010 that farmers of the village use mostly tubewell for irrigating the crops. Most of the farmers having more than one tubewells therefore due to deeper groundwater level almost all the existing open wells are defunct. The soils of the village is deep soil, which is very fertile, but most of the farmers cultivate chickpea due to scarcity of the irrigation water despite good rainfall, the water availability from the tubewell is gradually reduced after the month of December. Therefore, it was estimated that if the runoff from the cultivated field is collected at a suitable location it will not only increase the *rabi* crop productivity but also will provide life saving irrigation to *kharif* crops during prolonged dry spell. Thus by storing the runoff water at suitable location in individual farmer's field can diversify the *rabi* crops by including potato, onion, garlic and wheat in place of chickpea, besides increasing productivity. Initially the farmers of the village were reluctant to construct water harvesting tank because it is hypnotized that due to tank construction a sizable part of land would be wasted and will not be in use for crop cultivation. The continuous persuasion and attempts by the team, ultimately was successful in convincing a farmer Shri Balu Singh s/o Nathu Singh for the construction of water harvesting tank in his field.

In March 2011, a suitable site was located in the existing drainage line for the construction of water harvesting tank in the field of Shri Balu Singh. For this purpose, a JCB machine for 150 hours was provided from project side on participatory approach. The excavated soil was lifted using two dumpers and was used for levelling the field of Shri Balu Singh and other farmers. The cost of two dumpers was born by the farmer. By this way Shri Balu Singh not only recovered the cost of hiring dumpers by selling the excavated soil to other farmers but also brought a sizable portion of his undulating field to levelled condition. In this manner in March 2011 itself, a tank of storage capacity of 1400 m^3 was constructed. The collected runoff water stored during rainy season of 2011 and filled to its full capacity.

The stored water was used by Balu Singh during *kharif* and *rabi* season. The emptied tank was refilled by the farmer'sby using tubewell. This way Balu Singh continue to use surface and groundwater in conjunction. Since 2011 onwards to till date the tank is getting filled continuously by runoff and the farmer using ground and surface water appropriately.

Before the Tank Construction

Before the tank construction Shri Balu Singh was cultivating soybean with an average production of 12 q/ha during *rabi* and chickpea was being planted with an average yield 6 q/ha. even some time no crop could be cultivated successfully for the want of sufficient irrigation water.

After the Tank Construction

Through participatory approach, a tank of 1400 m^3 capacity was constructed under NICRA Project during 2011 in the field of Shri Balu Singh. The site for the tank was selected in such way that the natural drainage line is not obstructed but after filling tank should continue drain of excess water naturally. Similarly, it was ensured that the field of Shri Balu Singh does not get inundate after filling the tank and excess water from the tank does not initiate soil erosion in downstream field. In March 2011, the tank was constructed and it got filled in June 2011 itself. The stored water was used for irrigating the *kharif* crops as lifesaving irrigation during prolonged dry spell. This enhances the productivity of soybean by 10 q/ha in the field of Shri Balu Singh, In comparison to that of other farmers in September 2011. The tank got refilled with runoff water which was again used for pre-sowing irrigation to 1.75 ha field. After using the stored water, the tank was refilled with tubewell water. This way the conjunctive use of stored run off water and tubewell water, the farmer could provide pre-sowing irrigation to 03 ha field with chickpea (Dollar) and second irrigation after 15-20 days crop stage. This way after the construction water harvesting structure the farmers could provide 18q/ ha chickpea (dollar) which was three times more than the chickpea production before the construction of water harvesting tank. The dollar chickpea also ensured higher income in comparison to desi variety of chickpea. Thus, it is very clear that the construction of tank was benefited Balu singh for enhancing crop production and farm income (Table 1.1).

Table 1.1: Change in Cropping Pattern Before and After the Tank Construction

Particulars	*Before the Tank Construction*	*After the Tank Construction*
Soybean	12q/ha -lower productivity	22 q/ha -higher productivity
Onion	Not sown	100q (0.25ha) -2011
	Not sown	300q (0.75ha) -2013
Garlic	Not sown	Start cultivation
Potato	Not sown	Start cultivation
Chickpea	6q/ha (desi)	18 q/ha dollar
Fallow during *Rabi*	1 ha	None
Pre-sowing irrigation	None	1.75ha

In 2013 Shri Balu Singh started cultivation of onion in 0.25ha besides cultivation chickpea (dollar). He harvested almost 100 q onion in 2013. Since 2014 onwards, he is cultivating onion in 0.75 ha land and harvested 300 q onion and earning additional farm income. Before the construction of water harvesting tank, Balu singh invested for number of borings to get tubewell water but was not successful in getting appreciable amount of groundwater and lost handsome amount for these unsuccessful attempts. During the construction of tank the excavated soil was use by him for making his field leveled and for enhancing its fertility. On the other hand, the excess excavated soil was sold by him to other farmers for spreading into their fields. This way he earned a sum of Rs. 53100 by selling the excavated soil and helped him directly and indirectly in many ways (Table 12). After the construction of the tank and its filling by runoff water the tubewell also getting recharged and providing more water than earlier. Since 2012 onwards, Shri Balu Singh is utilizing the harvested water for irrigating *kharif* and *rabi* crops and again refilling it with tubewell water for efficient irrigation as gradually reducing discharge from tubewell November onward is not able to provide sufficient irrigation and cover the cultivated fields if provided directly. This way by storing tubewell water in the tank, it is utilized for irrigation purpose using high discharge pump.

Table 1.2: Direct Indirect Benefits of the Tank Construction

Particulars	*Before the Tank Construction*	*After the Tank Construction*
Storage of tubewell water	Not possible	Possible
Excess runoff water storage	Not possible	Possible
Conjunctive use of surface and groundwater	Not possible	Possible
Excavated soil	Not available	Spread in the field and sold to other farmers and earned 53100/-
Soil fertility	-	Enhanced
Levelling land	Undulation	Possible
Lifesaving irrigation during prolonged dry spells for *kharif* crops from runoff water	Was not possible	Possible
Investment for borewell/tubewell	Lot of amount	Nil
Nearby tubewell	never recharge and have lesser water	Fully recharged and have sufficient water
Soil erosion	Continued	Reduced and controlled
Recharge of tubewell	not possible	Possible and increased

Thus, it can be concluded that the decision of Shri Balu Singh to go for construction of water harvesting tank was very much beneficial to him and has become a source of motivation and inspiration for other farmers and helped him directly and indirectly. Similarly, the hypothesis that with construction of tank in a portion of cultivated field is not beneficial proved to be wrong and invalid. This is a success story of farmer who is not only storing the runoff water but also diversifying the cropping pattern successfully through conjunctive use of surface and groundwater for efficient irrigation. The stored water is used for providing lifesaving irrigation to *kharif* crop during prolonged dry spell and for providing supplemental irrigation to *rabi* crops.

BALARAM TANK 2011
44 M * 23 M * 4.4 M DEEP
NICRA
NINGNOTI 2011
06/07/2011

BALARAM TANK
44 M*23 M* 4.4 M DEEP
NINGNOTI 2011
07/26/2011

BALARAM TANK
44 M*23 M* 4.4 M DEEP
SIDE SLOPE STABLISHED
NINGNOTI 2011
11/26/2011

Refilled water harvesting tank
NINGNOTI 2018
11.5.2018

Balaam tank constructed in 2011
NINGNOTI 2018
20.3.2018

Refilled by tubewell water
NINGNOTI 2018
20.3.2018

Onion in 1 ha area
NINGNOTI 2018
20.3.2018

Tank as storage tank for irrigating Onion in 1 ha area
NINGNOTI 2018
20.3.2018

Cultivated field after harvest of Onion
NINGNOTI 2018
11.5.2018

Cultivated field after harvest of Onion and storage of onion in field
NINGNOTI 2018
11.5.2018

Onion storage after harvesting
NINGNOTI 2018
11.5.2018

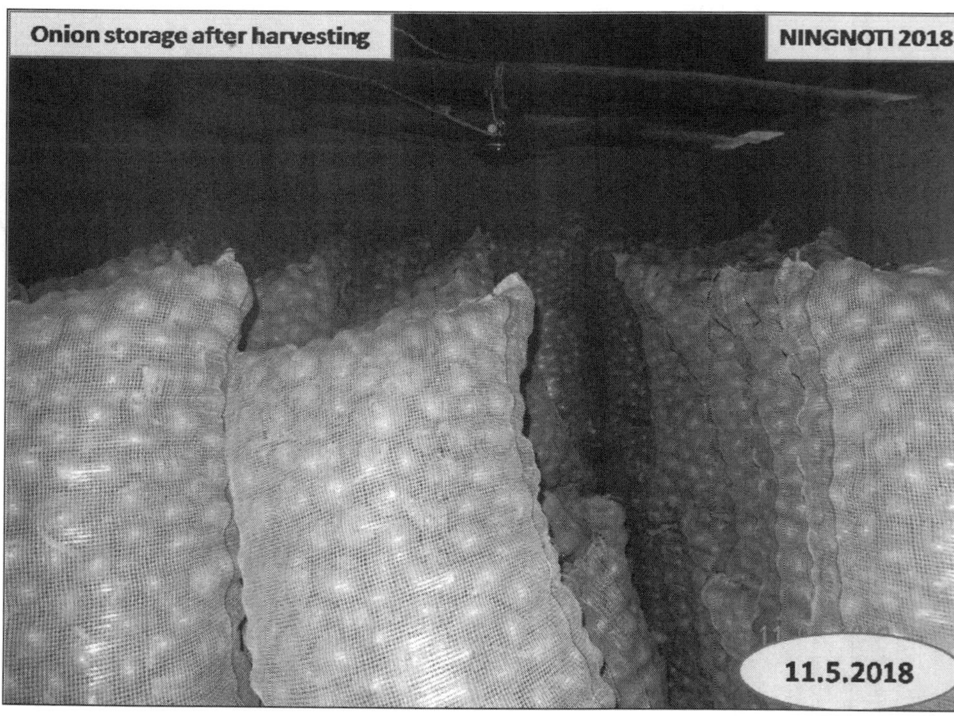
Onion storage after harvesting
NINGNOTI 2018
11.5.2018

Chapter 2

Innovative and Efficient Water Management Practice for Irrigating *Rabi* Crops through Harvested Water in Malwa Region

During 2007-2008, a village Shriram Panod (district Indore) was selected by the team of ***Operational Research Project for Dryland Agriculture, College of Agriculture, RVSKVV Campus Indore*** to achieve the major objectives of the project. It was observed in the village and from the information gathered through PRA exercise that due to non-availability of groundwater, lot of area could not be brought under cultivation during *rabi* season many a times in this village. Further, it is assessed that the runoff potential of the soils (Vertisols) of the area is very high due to their low infiltration rate. The safe disposal/storage of this runoff would be beneficial. The storage of the runoff water would help the farmer to utilize it during the moisture stress period. Thus attempts should be made to enhance the water availability in the farmer's fields. With this objective in view, it is therefore, decided to increase the runoff water storage in the selected farmer's field (Shri Dharmendra Bhagwat Singh Chouhan) which is otherwise runs out of the field after creating sheet erosion losses and development of washes.

Construction of Excavated Water Harvesting Tank

A suitable site in his field was selected considering all the hydrological aspects in January 2008 and an excavated tank was developed in March 2008 through participatory approach. The idea was mainly to provide the technical guidance and sharing the cost to the tune of 50 per cent from the project side and to motivate the farmers for devoting a portion of his land for the construction of tank besides 50 per cent cost so that the stored water could be utilized during the stress period. Before the site selection, it was ensured that the site retains the water without causing any appreciable losses in the storage. For this purpose, back hoe loader machines was used for the excavation purpose and dumper were used for transporting and spreading the excavated only top black soil (available up to 2 m) in the nearby fields which was severely affected by rill and sheet erosion process. The farmers then engaged the tractor drawn levellers for spreading the excavated materials and making the fields almost levelled. The yellowish soil excavated beyond 2m was also used for the construction of side bunds and peripheral bunds of the farmers and also for the construction of farm roads. The inlet of the tank was provided on the either side bund facing the cultivated field. The outlet was also constructed so that it safely drains off the excess water into a natural waterway so that the excavated tank would collect the runoff water in the forthcoming rainy season, which could be utilized during the stress period for irrigating the crops. The other details are as follows:

Catchment area: 20 ha, **Storage capacity:** 0.55 ha.m, **Maximum depth:** 2.85 m

The excavated tank collected the runoff water in the following rainy season in 2008 and farmer also filled it with available groundwater in the nearby tubewell as its discharge was not sufficient enough to be used directly for pre-sowing irrigation through the border. Subsequently three irrigations to wheat grown in 4 ha and one irrigation to chick pea in 2 ha was provided through the conjunctive use of surface and groundwater stored in the tank in the first year itself. Since then every year, the tank is getting filled with the runoff water and the stored water was used mainly during the *rabi* season for providing irrigations to adjoining crops. The available water in the tank gave so much confidence in the farmer (Shri Dharmendra Bhagwat Singh Chouhan) that he brought more area under wheat which requires more irrigation.

Refilling of Tank with Tubewell Water

Generally in this region, the tubewells provide groundwater with reduced discharge after the termination of monsoon season as groundwater depletes at faster rate due to overexploitation. Therefore,very few tubewells operate throughout the year otherwise most of the tubewells go dry or supply water only for 2-3 hours that too with very reduced quantity. At the same time, electric power supply is a deterrent in providing continuous irrigation to field's crops. Sometimes the supply of tubewell is so less that direct irrigation is not possible as water advancement process does not take place particularly in medium and deep clayey soils due to cracking pattern and irrigation process is not completed despite pump running for several hours. Therefore, after using the harvested water for pre-sowing irrigation during 2009, the farmer also started refilling this water harvesting tank with nearby tubewell water and then using it for irrigating the nearby fields using a high discharge diesel/ electric pump so that a larger area can be irrigated at a time. Thus the farmer rely more on stored water in the tank than the tubewell water as most of the tubewells dry up suddenly/abruptly due to groundwater depletion.

Construction of Water Harvesting Tank in Panod (2008).

Excavation of Water Harvesting Tank.

Spreading Excavated Soil in the Fields for Increasing Fertility and Levelling the Field.

Use for Harvested Water for Irrigating *Rabi* Crops.

Filled Tank Due to Heavy Runoff in Post Monsoon Season on 14.11.2009.

Filled Tank on 20.07.2010 Due to Runoff in Monsoon Season.

Using Runoff Water on 19.10.2010 for Pre-sowing Irrigation.

Refilling with Ground Eater 12.11.2010.

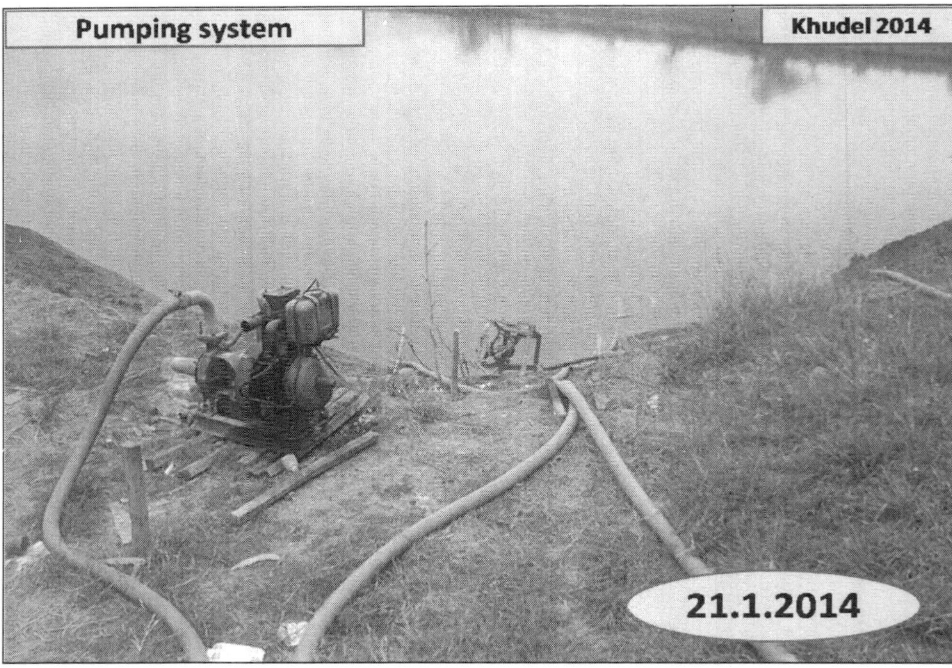

Use of both Diesel and Electric Pump for Irrigation.

Arrangement for Refilling the Tank with Tubewell Water.

Arrangement of Typical Pumping Unit

The stored water in the water harvesting tank allowed the farmer (Shri Dharmendra Bhagwat Singh Chouhan) to use some innovative ideas mainly for

Use of Generator.

Typical Pumping Unit Arrangements for Irrigating *Rabi* Crops (2010-2011).
Use of Y shaped connectors to connect diesel and electric pumps to main pipe line.

10/19/2010

10/19/2010

10/19/2010

efficient utilization of harvested water and use of harvested tank very effectively. Since the time electric power supply is a deterrent in providing continuous irrigation to field's crops, in 2010, he made a typical water pumping arrangement for lifting water from the water harvesting tank and irrigating the adjoining fields without interruption. For this purpose, he made the provision of submersible horizontal pump (locally known as Pandubbi) and diesel pump connected to main supply pipe line through Y shaped connectors so that the water can be pumped using either of the pumping unit. In the absence of electric power supply, the fields are irrigated using diesel pump. A generator is also provided for lifting the water with both diesel and electric pump simultaneously in the absence of electric power supply. Further, the farmer also started collecting the tubewell water this tank (after the use of harvested water mainly for pre-sowing irrigation) for few days and then the stored water is used for irrigating the nearby fields using a high discharge diesel/ electric pump so that a larger area can be irrigated at a time. This provision of typical water pumping unit ensured the timely and uninterrupted irrigation of *rabi* crops and thus helped the farmer to enhance his productivity and farm income.

Traditional Methods of Sowing and Irrigation of *Rabi* Crops

Traditionally in Malwa region, *rabi* crops are sown in two ways:

1. Land preparation is carried out for *rabi* sowing after *kharif* crop harvesting. The prepared fields are provided pre-sowing irrigation through flood

Dry Sowing and then Border Formation Using Tractor Drawn Bund Former.

Furrow on above all Borders for Carrying Water to be Delivered in Borders.

Bund Former for making Borders after Sowing of *Rabi* Crops.

Bund Forming Arrangement for making Borders along with *Rabi* Crop Sowing.

method and then sowing of *rabi* crops by seed drill is carried out. In the sowed field, borders (preferably 6 feet wide) are formed using bund former along the field slope for providing subsequent irrigations to the cropped field as per the availability of water and requirement of the crops. This practice is adopted when monsoon is terminated early and soil becomes dry and deep cracks are formed in the fields. The fields are irrigated through wild flooding and uneven distribution of irrigation water affects the germination.

2. In second method, dry sowing of *rabi* crops are carried out after land preparation and then borders are formed along the field slope for providing irrigation as per the crop requirement and water availability. This practice is followed when sufficient moisture is available in the soil profile due to late withdrawal of monsoon or higher rainfall which allows dry sowing. Better irrigation water distribution is possible in this practice due to border irrigation as water moves in strips which ensure better and uniform germination in the field.

In traditional border irrigation system during *rabi* season, many farmers pump the water and release directly into the border using flexible rubber pipes. In case of direct release of water through pipe in the border, faster movement of

Direct Pumping of Water into Border using Flexible Pipe.

Sheet Erosion due to High Discharge Affects the Germiantion Too.

Uncontrolled Water Movement and Stagnation at the End of Border.

Manual Attention is Required Otherwise over Irrigation and Submergence of Crop at the End of the Border is Common. Sometime water moves out off the field and wastage of water is observed in many cases particularly in night hours.

water front takes place and it requires much attention to avoid water wastage. However, uncontrolled delivery of water in border cause sheet erosion and affects the germination and water gets stagnate at the end of the border and moves out the border.

In another practice, irrigation water is pumped through PVC pipe and left into a furrow formed at the upper portion of bordered field for carrying water from first border to last border. The furrow in the upper portion carries the water till end with reduced water conveyance efficiency (in the range of 60 to 75 per cent depending upon soil profile moisture condition). Water is then released into various borders one by one from this furrow and it is controlled manually by opening and blocking the bunds using spade continuously during pumping hours. If it is not done attentively, uncontrolled and over-irrigation due to high discharge rate damages the borders and germination is affected. Thus, border irrigation is a labour and time consuming work and it requires experienced and devoted skilled labour for better and efficient irrigation.

Further, in this region, it is observed that due to peak hour requirement of electric power, electricity is supplied in the villages in two shifts *i.e.* five hours each in day and night respectively during *rabi* season. Obviously, particularly during night hours, it is impossible and very tedious to be in the fields' whole night for irrigating the crops in unbearable cold. Therefore, the farmers normally put the pump on till the electric power is available and allow the water at higher pumping discharge rate to move in the fields on their own through pipes without attending it all the time. This system not only over irrigates the fields but also wastes the precious water and allows it to move out of the fields without covering the maximum possible fields under irrigation.

Innovative and Efficient Water Management and Saving System for Irrigating *Rabi* Crops

To avoid the chances of over irrigation and wastage of precious irrigation water and also to save labour and time, it was thought during 2015 that if acontrolled system is used so that discharge is reduced and regulated in each border so that water moves uniformly in various borders. Similarly, it will be beneficial if the number of borders to be irrigated simultaneously can be increased or reduced as per the power supply schedule without over irrigation and wastage of water. Further, it is also required to make the arrangements for regulating the water in each border depending upon the soil moisture profile. It is observed that when sufficient moisture is available in the soil profile, water moves faster into the borders otherwise in dry profile, it moves very slowly. Thus as per the requirement, the water flow and movement can be regulated and number of borders to be irrigated can be enhanced or reduced. Further, it is also desirable that after setting the system, personal attention and presence in the field is not required continuously.

Keeping the objectives and points in view, in 2106 Mr. Dharmendra Bhagwat Singh Chouhan, Village and Post Office: Shriram Panod, district Indore (M.P.) has made arrangement for irrigating the chickpea or wheat grown in borders in consultation with ORP team members.

Wild Flooding for Pre-sowing Irrigation.

Pre-Sowing Irrigation.

Border irrigation after Dry Sowing.

Water is Pumped and Left in Furrow Formed above the Borders and then Released in Borders Manually through Bund Opening and Closing by using Spade.

11/07/2008

10/29/2013

Water is Pumped using Diesel or Electric Pump from the Water Harvesting Tank.

In this system, a main PVC pipe line (consisting of various pipes of 20 feet each, 75 mm diameter pipe each) is laid along the head of borders in the entire cropped field to carry the irrigation water from the water source (in the present case it is water harvesting tank) till the upper portion of last border near field boundary thus ensuring higher water conveyance efficiency (almost 100 per cent).

In main pipeline, the end pipe is kept closed using a cap so that irrigation water can not be delivered directly in the border through pipe. Significantly in this system, only PVC pipe mainline is laid and thus no provision of a water carrying furrow is made which is otherwise formed in traditional system through which water is diverted manually into various borders. Provision of end cap and no formation of furrow also restrict the wastage of water and avoid any damage to borders and crops due to sheet erosion.

Further, in each pipe of 20 feet, three openings of one inch diameter each at 6 feet interval are provided and valve system is attached to it to regulate and control the water flow for irrigating borders of six feet wide. Thus, due to provision of valve, discharge in the each border can be controlled by opening and closing the valve. Normally six valves are used at a time for irrigating six borders individually. Initially an assessment is to made by considering soil moisture profile,water front advancement in the border and duration of irrigation which can be given without physical attention in the field to calculate the time required in irrigating entire border

Main Pipe Line from the Water Source till the Field Boundary and above all Borders.

End of the Main Pipe Line Tightly Closed using a Cap.

length. Then the discharge rate is fixed in all the valves to facilitate and ensure uniform and simultaneous water front movement in all the six borders. Thus, as per the calculated time required time for irrigating entire border, the attendant can come to stop the delivery of water in all six borders and can make arrangements for irrigating the next six borders in row. The position of all these valves are kept facing upward so that kinetic energy of water is dissipated and no sheet erosion takes place in borders. Normally, six valves are used for irrigating six borders individually. However, the number of openings can be increased or decreased depending upon the soil profile moisture in the borders. For first irrigation, only six valves are used as soil moisture profile is relatively dry. However, in subsequent irrigations, the water front moves very fast with same discharge in each border due to relatively wet soil moisture profile than that of the initial irrigation. Thus, the number of openings can be increased up to twelve to irrigate twelve borders by regulating the valves.

Controlling valves are also provided in main lines after 60 feet so that by using these valves, flow in the main pipe line beyond that point can be regulated or restricted for maintaining the desired pressure and discharge in each individual border by opening or closing the valve in main line.

Valve System of 1 inch at a Distance of 6 Feet in all PVC Pipes (3 valves in each pipe).

Each Valve System in Main Pipe Line to be Delivered in each Border – Flow can be Regulated using Valve.

Controlling and Regulating Flow in Borders to be Irrigated and Already Irrigated by Opening and Closing Valves. Valvés are kept facing upward to reduce the chances of sheet erosion in borders.

Controlling and regulating the flow in main pipeline and borders already irrigated.
Panod 2017
24.10.2017

Valves in Main Line at a Distance of 60 feet are also Provided to Control and Regulate Flow to Maintain Pressure in the Portion where Irrigation is to be Provided in Various Borders.

Irrigating many Borders at a Time. Uniform Movement of Water Front in all Borders.

Thus, by using this innovative and efficient water management device, it is observed that the use of the system not only allows uniform water front movement in the entire border being irrigated simultaneously, but also saves labour, time and the wastage of water. Further the regulated and controlled delivery of water in border avoids the chances of sheet erosion and water stagnation at the end of borders, ensuring better germination.

Advantage of the System

1. The water flow and movement can be regulated and number of borders to be irrigated can be enhanced or reduced.
2. The system avoids the over irrigation and wastage of precious irrigation water
3. Water moves uniformly in various borders
4. Number of borders to be irrigated simultaneously can be increased or reduced as per the power supply schedule.
5. Personal attention and presence in the field is not required continuously.
6. Can be run whole night during electric power availability without attending the system.
7. The discharge rate can be regulated and various borders can be irrigated simultaneously.
8. Can be made in local workshop.
9. Very useful under limited power supply at night.
10. Dependency on the labour can be reduced.

Thus, by using the system (device), it can be clearly pointed out that the border irrigation is no more labour and time consuming work and can be operated by unskilled labour with better and efficient irrigation. It is to be highlighted that many farmers of the region visiting his farm and trying to use such useful innovative idea in their fields too. Further it is to inform that this innovative idea came only after the construction of water harvesting tank in his field through one ICAR funded project by ORP team. The availability of the water in the tank gave him confidence and only then this innovative idea came in his mind during the discussion at the site. It is not to mention here that water harvesting tank not only collects the runoff water but also can be used as storage tank for collecting tubewell water for its timely and efficient use. The increased water availability not only increases the crop productivity and farm income but it also gives confidence in the farmer to allow him to do experiments on various aspects of crop and water management.

Chapter 3

Effectiveness and Utility of Percolation Tanks in Malwa and Nimar Region

As per the objectives of All India Coordinated Research Project for Dryland Agriculture, College of Agriculture, Indore, the project team have been visiting different villages of various districts of Malwa and Nimar region to have live contacts with the farmers.Initially during 1990, when it was desired to assess farmers's priority and problems related to agricultural activities, all the time it was demanded by the farmers that project should attempt to increase the irrigation water availability in the area and should provide improved varieties of different crops so that agriculture production can be enhanced. Through various watershed programmes, many water harvesting tanks were constructed mostly on government lands for providing irrigation water to farmers. The improved varieties of different crops like soybean, chickpea, maize *etc.* enhanced the farm productivity and income with the help of supplemental water through water harvesting tanks. During 2000 onwards, with the success stories of these water harvesting tanks,number of farmers got convinced, inspired and provided their own lands to the project for the construction of water harvesting tanks on it. This process helped these farmers to grow successful *rabi* crops like chickpea, wheat, potato, onion and garlic after *kharif*.

After all these interventions from project side, it was experienced by the team that in Malwa region several geographical situations are existed where water harvesting tanks could not be constructed as on these locations, the cultivated fields are underlained by fragmented basalt which is having very high percolation rate and thus the runoff could be collected and stored for longer time. Therefore, the farmers having these type of situations were not agreed to construct percolation tank instead of water harvesting tank because they wished to have surface stored water for irrigation. Though they were agreeing to the fact that percolation tank construction would enhance the groundwater recharge, which can ultimately can provide increased irrigation water through their tubewells and open wells. Thus, they did not want the construction of percolation tank in their field as it make a part of their cultivated field.

During 1991, at the lowest boundary of College of Agriculture, Indore, a percolation tank was constructed with the provision of gabion structure at outlet. The tank is collecting huge amount of runoff as per its capacity and then draining the excess water safely into the natural drain. The stored water is continuously getting percolated and this process is repeated number of times during entire rainy season. The immediate impact of this tank can be seen in the adjoining open well which has started providing irrigation water almost throughout the year since then.

In 2000, the project identified a land portion, which was adjoining the ridgeline of the field of Shri S.C.Sharma of village Baroli district Indore. The runoff water from the ridgeline used to enter with the high velocity in field of Shri Sharma and was eroding the parts of cultivated field and thereby damaging the crops and retarding the fertility. The project constructed a 190m long and 2m wide earthen bund in this wasteland by using a bulldozer. Because of this activity, the degraded and wasted land adjoining the ridgeline was converted into tank area, which immediately started collecting the runoff water in the upstream site of the earthen bund. This helped to reduce the losses in the cultivated field due to soil erosion completely and to collect huge amount of runoff water in the wasted portion. Since the soil was underlain by basaltic murram, the stored water was percolated within few days. During 2000 monsoon season itself, this tank area were filled several time with runoff and were percolated. These resulted in the enhanced water availability in the nearby stepwell and other openwells located in the fields of Shri Sharma. These open wellswere recharged fully and filled up to the brim, which was otherwise an impossible situation inthis village. Due to percolation tank the 10 ha area could be irrigated with high productivity and income from chickpea and wheat productionduring *rabi* season.Though Shri Sharma was involved in agriculture activities for 25 years,he was able to irrigate only 0.75 ha land using open well water before the percolation tank construction. Since 2000 onward, he has been irrigating *rabi* crops due to enhanced water availability due to construction of percolation tank. Now he is a successful and resourceful farmer and his experience with percolation tank is inspiring many other farmers.

In 2005 also, a percolation tank was constructed by the projectusing bulldozer in a field adjoining to ridgeline in the village Jaitpura block Sanwer district Indore. In the first year itself, a huge amount of runoff was collected in the tank area that enhanced the recharge of nearby open well and tubewell. The storage of runoff water in the upper portion also helped in reducing the soil erosion losses in the lower fields.

In 2008, a progressive farmer Shri Keval Singh Patel from village Hatod, tehsil Depalpur District Indore contacted the project team and requested to construct water-harvesting tank through technical guidance. The project team observed that after the construction of tank, it would not be possible to retain the stored water for longer time as this portion is underlained by basaltic murram that is having very high percolation rate. When this was informed to Shri Patel, he was very distressed initially because he wanted to have water harvesting tank. However he agreed to get constructed percolation tank in this portion. With the help of technical guidance from project team, Shri Patel invested Rs 3 lakhs for the construction of a big percolation tank.Actually this portion of land of Shri Patel was adjoining to a ridgeline and was severely affected by soil erosion. The uncontrolled runoff water from this portion was badly damaging his land and crops. In this natural drain line, he initially tried to adopt different measures like loose boulder structures to control the runoff. However because of high velocity of runoff, he could not be able to do so. The project team constructed a percolation tank of size 80x30x2 m in the natural drain line which is now not only collecting the runoff but also completly reduced the chances of heavy damage in the lower portion of the fields. This stored water collected during rainy season since 2008 onward, is getting percolated and recharging nearby open well and tubewells. Because of this, even *rabi* crops is being grown successfully in most of the cultivated fields which was otherwise impossible befor the construction of percolation tank. Shri Patel got so overwhelmed with the success of percolation tank in the first year itself and he thanked the team several times. He also admitted that only because of team members, he got convinced for the construction of percolation tank which is not only helping him through subsurface storage of runoff water but also helping other farmers to save their fields from the soil erosion losses and helping their tubewells for getting recharged. Further, he is proud to solve the problem of uncontrolled runoff technically and also helping the other farmers socially.

In 2000, the project team helped technically to an NGO for the construction of a big percolation tank in the village Hathuniya, tehsil Sanwer district Indore, which collects a huge amount of runoff and provides it to an opportunity to get percolated every monsoon since then. This has also been found very effective in controlling the losses through uncontrolled runoff. This percolation tank also collecting runoff water and helping it to get stored underground, thus resulting regular recharge of nearby tubewells and open wells. This tank also collecting the runoff water that was otherwise moving into river kshipra after damaging various cultivated fields located in its natural drain line. The immediate effect of this percolation tank reflected in the tubewell and open well located in tank area itself,that started providing groundwater even during summer season which is very rare and impossible phenomena.

In 2010, a percolation tank (2500m^3) was constructed by a farmer Shri M.K. Patidar in village Panod block Sanwer district Indore under the technical guidance of AICRPDA team. The farmer also provided two shafts for ensuring deeper percolation of the stored runoff water through these shafts which were provided with metallic filter material to avoid the entry of foreign materials in groundwater. The immediate effect of this activity realized in the following monsoon season and several runoff events filled the tank many times and allowed to get percolated through basaltic murram and even with the shafts.This activity recharged the nearby two tubewells, which provided sufficient irrigation water for the irrigation to *rabi* crops in almost 10 ha area. This phenomenon is still happening and providing sufficient irrigation water through tubewells even during scanty rainfall period.

Similarly the team visited village Lonsara tehsil Rajpura district Barwani in the year 2014 for assessing the problems and providing technical guidance to village farmers. The team observed that in between two ridgelines, an earthen dam was constructed in 1990which is collecting and storing huge amount of water and providing irrigation water through canal in various villages for irrigation which has been found very helpful in increasing the crop productivity. However the effect of dam can be observed in few villages where canal are not provided but the tubewells and open wells are providing sufficient irrigation water even during summer season. Actually before the construction of dam, a seasonal river used to flow naturally through these villages. The amount of flowing water in this river drastically reduced after the construction of earthen dam at the starting point. However instead of flowing water the quantity of subsurface water in this river belt increased in its 10km long river bed. In this portion, the farmers constructed more than 100 open wells at regular interval and surprisingly in each openwell, groundwater is available within 2-3 m from ground level. Due to availability of appreciable amount of irrigation water, these villages can be seen growingmultiple crops with wide range of crop diversity. Even during summer season due to enhanced groundwater, farmers are growing maize, tomato, cucumber, watermelon and various vegetablessuccessfully, which was otherwise not possible in these village despite locating on the bank of seasonal river. Even the submersible pumps of few tubewells are replaced by centrifugal pumps as groundwater are available within 3-4m from ground level. This way, it can be experienced that the construction of earthen dam is not only helpful in providing irrigation water through canals but also providing subsurface water through open wells and tubewells in sufficient quantity for various crops grown during *kharif*, *rabi* and summer season even in canal free villages.

In March 2018 in the research field of AICRPDA, a percolation tank of 907 m^3 storage capacity was constructed. This percolation tank was so constructed that it not only receives excess water from the HDPE lined water harvesting tank but also collects the runoff from other agricultural field.The soil of the area is underlained by basaltic murram which is having 18-20 cm percolation rate per day.Therefore the stored water in the percolation tank continuous gets percolated which ultimately enhances the chances of groundwater recharge. Before the construction of this percolation tank, the excess water from lined water harvesting tank and runoff water from other areas continuously eroding the lower portions of farm area due to higher velocity of runoff water.Immediately after the construction of percolation tank, the excess runoff water is stored in the percolation tank which ultimately controlling the soil erosion and its adverse effect in appreciable farm area. This way in AICRPDA research field not only runoff water is being collected in lined water harvesting tank (1781m^3) but also the runoff water is stored in percolation tank for its ultimate utilization for groundwater recharge. Thus rainwater is properly being managed for its further utilization during *kharif* and *rabi* season and thus reducing the losses to offsite fields due to soil erosion.

Construction of Percolation Tank.

Tank Underlained by Basaltic Murrum.

Runoff Water in Percolation Tank.

HDPE Lined Water Harvesting Tank.

Lined and Unlined Tanks.

Stored Water in Lined and Unlined Tank.

Lined and Unlined Tank.

Percolation Tank.

Percolation Tank Reduced the Offsite Damage to Cultivated Fields.

Deepening in Gullied Portion in between Stop Dam.

Recharging of Open Well due to Sunken Pond.

Basaltic Murrum does not Allow Storage of Water for Longer Time.

Diversion Bund Stored Runoff Water on Upstream Site to get Percolated.

Construction of Percolation Tank Adjoining to Ridgeline.

Percolation Tank Allowed Recharging and Reduced Off-site Damage to Fields.

Fully Rechrged Stepwell.

Storage of Runoff in Percolation Tank with the Help of Earthen Bund.

Recharged Open Well.

Percolation Tank in the Portion Adjoining to Ridgeline.

Big Percolation Stores Huge Amount of Runoff and Recharge the Groundwater.

Percolation Tank Allowed Recharging and Reduced off-site Damage to Fields.

Groundwater Available within 2-3 m in Open Well due to Percolation or Seepage.

Subsurface Percolation Recharging the Open Well Constructed in River Bed.

Recharged Tubewell Use of Centrifugal Pump in Place of Submersible Pump.

Various village panchayats of different villages constructed stopdams in gullied portion which resulted in stabilization of gullies and make it possible to drain of runoff water safely for enhancing water availability in the village. The AICRPDA project organized a training programme to different watershed committees in 2016. In this training programme, the technological guidance was provided so that the area between two stop dams in the stabilized gullied culd be excavated to construct sunken pond in the series. It was also suggested that the excavated soil should be spread into unleveled field or in wasted land so that crop production can be enhanced. Shri lokendra singh tomar village Harsola, block Mhow District Indore adopted this suggestion and constructed sunken pond in the gullied portion and used the excavated soil to make a new field to make it suitablefor crop cultivation. The immediate impact of this was seen in the area which was totally dry on 20.06.2018 for the want of monsoonic rain, was full of water on 22.06.2018 in the first rainy shower itself. This portion immediately served as a percolation tank and recharged the nearly open well to convert it into an irrigation source which was otherwise not possible at all. During the entire monsoon season of 2018, this situationwas seen throughout the season that the sunken pond retained huge amount of runoff water and converted it into subsurface water through recharging the open well. Similarly the huge amount of runoff water retained in portion between the two stop dams which ultimately reduced the losses in the cultivated fields located on the downstream sides.

The success stories generated from all above-mentioned percolation tanks, many farmers are getting motivated and contacting the project team for providing technical guidance for the construction of percolation tank in their fields, which was otherwise a rare gesture. Based on the experiences gathered from all the percolation tanks, it can be pointed out that these tanks are very useful in storing the runoff and recharging the groundwater and even controlling the erosion losses to offsite field located on downstream site. This way percolation tank is considered at par with water harvesting tank in terms of enhancing availability of irrigation water.

Chapter 4

Successful Approach for Integrated Farming System

Team of scientists from All India Coordinated Research Project for Dryland Agriculture, College of Agriculture, Indore regularly visits different rural areas for convincing and motivating the farmers for adopting improved rainfed technologies for enhancing their farm production and income. During a visit to Dhar district of Malwa and Nimar region, the team came across few progressive farmers who are practicing various agricultural methods on basis of their own field experiences for earning profits from farming. However, due to lack of extension activities and awareness, other farmers are not getting information on these very successful and efficient farming practices. An experience gathered by the team and shared by a progressive farmer is being presented below for its wide scale adoption.

A progressive farmer Dr. R.S. Sikarwar after retiring from Govt. Science College, Barwaniis involved in agricultural activities in village Mehalgaon, block Chikhalda of district Dhar (M.P.). He is adopting various innovative practices and trying to enhance agricultural production from his parental cultivated fields. Dr. Sikarwar got a part of parental land and owing it since 1990. At that time, this field was very severely damaged, eroded and degraded due to uncontrolled runoff movement from undulating fields with multidirectional slope. Initially, he started constructing various earthen bunds at different locations to reduce the land erosion process. Then he tried to level the different fields using various types of farm machineries. Since the soil depth in these fields is very deep, he was successful in levelling the field very effectively. In1991, Teak plantation of 500 saplings was carried out by him in one-hectare area of this levelled field. Similarly, plantation of aonla in one hectare and mosambi(citrus limetta) in one hectare was also carried out simultaneously. At various locations, plantation of mango, jackfruit, palm (tadi), sapota (chikoo), papaya, guava, banana, coconut, sandal woods, aromatic and medicinal plants *etc.* was carried out as per the requirement and availability of land. In another part of the levelled field, plantation of 1100 custard apple plants was carried out during

2007-08. Since his field is located near the bank of river Narmada, the farmer was having sufficient amount of water for irrigating these fruit plants. In between, these plant rows, cultivation of soybean -maize during *kharif* and wheat-chickpea in *rabi* was also started by him in with time.

After 4-5 years of plantation of aonla and mosambi (citrus limetta), he started getting fruit production from these plants. Since these fruits were new to the area, he earned a handsome income and profit from selling it initially. However, after few years, the income from aonla drastically reduced as other farmers also started growing aonla in their fields. Initially the aonla was purchased at the rate of Rs.20 per kg by the local vendors but later, its selling price was reduced to only Rs. 2-3 per kg due increased production in the area. However the higher income, profit and production from mosambi (*Citrus limetta*) were continued for 10-12 years which helped him developing the cultivated fields further.

At present, he is getting very good production from the 1100 plants of custard apple which were planted in 2007-08. Dr. Sikarwar informed about custard apple plants that these require less water, less maintenance and provide higher production in short time. However, it is very essential to provide irrigation to these plants at the time of fruiting, which ensures very high production of custard apple. All these trees are being irrigated using drip irrigation system. Beside custard apple, mango, jackfruit, sapota, palm (tadi), banana, coconut, sandal woods, papaya and medicinal and aromatic products are also being sold by him in the nearby local market to add to the farm income.

The initial provision of earthen bunds brought the undulating fields to leveled conditions after few years. In these leveled fields, five farm ponds of 40X40X3 m size have been constructed. In these farm ponds, pumped seepage water from Narmada River and runoff during rainy season is being collected regularly by him. In these farm ponds, he started fish rearing and prawn production and even duckery.

Dr. Sikarwar was the professor of Zoology in local govt. Science College therefore he started using his own experiences and its application in his farm. In 2005, he got constructed cemented tanks of 10x10x2m in almost 4000 m^2 area. In these tanks, they are producing finger lings of various fishes. Good quality of compost cow dung manure is mixed in these cemented tanks to provide natural environment to all the fishes and also to provide feed for them. Dr. Sikarwar is producing fishes, prawns and earning higher income and profit from these rearing activities.

Dr. Sikarwar started innovative activities for the first time not only in Nimar region but also in Madhya Pradesh.He started producing pearl from these tanks, which were developed for fish rearing initially. For this purpose, he received practical training and technical knowledge from an institute at Bhubaneshwar. This training helped him for starting production of designer pearls instead of simple one. Though initially he faced lot of troubles for selling these pearls but after that he contacted traders from Hyderabad who helped him to earn a huge profit through the sell of designer pearls.

He is also practicing sericulture and moriculture since 2016. For this purpose, he planted shahtut (mulberry) plants in one hectare area and he is producing silk

Pearl production in farm ponds

Vermi-compost and agro-forestry

Pearl culture, pisciculture and prawn cultivation in farm ponds

Agro horti system with maize - aonla

Fish rearing along with fruit production

Medicinal and aromatic plants

Intercropping of papaya, banana and aonla

Fish rearing and duck production

Coconut and sandal wood plantation

Poultry farm with kadaknath

Fishery, pearl and lotus production

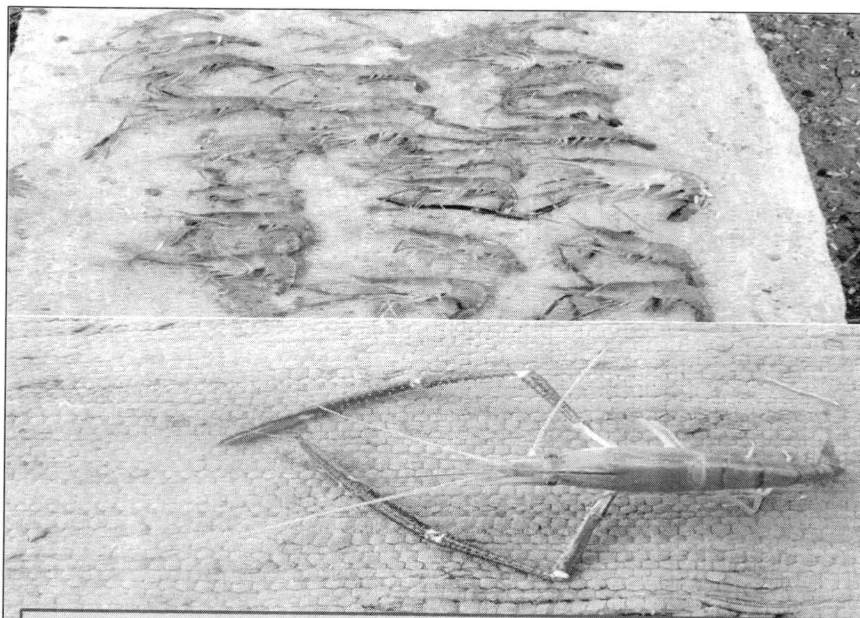

Prawn production

Cemented tanks for fish rearing

Water harvesting tanks for runoff collection

Pruning of mulberry trees

Plantation of mulberry trees

Fish production

Custard apple production

fiber. He ensured regular pruning and cutting of mulberry plants from time to time to allow their faster growth. Similarly, he tried for developing poultry business by having Kadaknath breed of birds. However, it is experienced by him that the Kadaknath bird is normally heavier than Broiler bird, therefore its production cost is also higher than Broiler. Therefore, production and selling of Broiler is easier than the Kadaknath breed.

In 2015-16, a vermi-compost unit was developed by using the leaves of teak plant, farm wastages and cow dung. For vermi-compost unit, he also tried and used plastic bags and cement separately. However it is suggested by him that cemented vermi-compost unit is cheaper and sustainable. It is also easier to collect vermi wash from cemented unit which can be used as liquid fertilizer along with drip system for irrigation purpose. He is also trying to develop various vermi-compost units in between rows of fully developed teak trees which were planted in 1991. The shades of the trees provide suitable environment for proper growth of worms by lowering the temperature as higher temperature always adversely affect worms working efficiency.

On the basis of experience shared by Dr. Sikarwar, it can be experienced that Dr. Sikarwar tried to adopt integrated farming system and also tried to enhance its quality from time to time to get higher farm production and income. He also shared that it is not easier to get higher income and production from any agricultural field because it is labourious and time consuming and requires higher input cost in the initial years. There are several years in which the farmers do not get the income but can incur losses in comparison to higher input cost. Similarly, farmers should adopt improved scientific technologies, improved varieties of crops and plants and improved techniques of irrigation gradually. He also wishes to suggest the farmers that after adopting any new technique, one should not expect immediate profit from it. Instead one should keep patience and should try for innovative ideas to enhance the income. Similarly in all the fields, soil and water conservation practices should be adopted for conserving natural resources for enhancing irrigation water availability for different crops and plants. The experiences shared by Dr. Sikarwar are worth considering and a source of inspiration for other farmers who wish to adopt integrated farming system by including other farm activities and enterprises for enhancing farm production and income on their own.

Chapter 5

Elevated Lined Water Storage Tank for Integrated Farming System

As per the requirement of AICRP on Dryland Agriculture, College of Agriculture, Indore, a team of scientists visited different villages to make the preliminary survey on the integrated farming systems being adopted by the farmers of the region during April- June 2018. While visiting Village Harsola block Mhow district Indore (N 22° 34.224′, E 75° 48.91′, 534 m elevation) the team came across a farmer Mr. Lokendra Rajput who shared his experiences on the farming situations and constraints faced by him. He also narrated about the steps taken and agricultural practices carried out by him and how he got motivated to make his farming into a profitable business by adopting improved water management technologies. His experiences are worth sharing and thus can motivate the others for its wide scale adoptability and enhancing the crop diversification and ultimately increasing the cropping intensity. The success story of the farmer also indicates that how the watershed programmes and watershed development activities undertaken through village panchayat can improve the farming situation through participatory approach.

Mr. Lokendra Rajput is involved actively in his farming since 1995 onward and his combined family owns about 10 ha cultivated fields. Since the village farms a part of Chambal river catchment, as the most of fields are having shallow to medium deep black soils underlain by basaltic murrum and then by hard stones with moderate slope in the range of 1 to 2 per cent due to the topographical situation of the village. Various types of erosion also created problems in his field like development of washes, small gullies and fragmentation of his fields. The uncontrolled runoff also developed serpentine shaped gullies on two sides of his field making the cultivation difficult in the cultivated fields. High amount of uncontrolled runoff also developed deep gully (20 m wide and irregular shaped with varying depths) nearby his fields in a stretch of 500 m on one side and a relatively smaller gully of size 10m wide and 200m length with irregular shaped with varying depths on other side. These two gullies used to drain off the water very quickly without providing any help for groundwater recharge.

Normally, he cultivates soybean, maize during *kharif* and mostly chickpea and potato in part during *rabi* season. He is having an open well which no longer provides irrigation water for last 20 years because of over exploitation of groundwater and lowering of groundwater table. Thus for providing irrigation to his crops particularly during *rabi* season, he dug up 11 tubewells from time to time at different locations so that he gets sufficient water for higher production of the crops. In spite of that, all the tubewells provide water only till the end of Decemebr and suddenly dry up and thus unable to provide irrigation during few critical stages of *rabi* crops thereby hampering the chances of producing satisfactory crop production. Thus, it can be pointed out that the scarcity of irrigation water had been his major constraint and concern for the existing farming system. Therefore, since 2015 he started very actively for enhancing water availability through proper rainwater management.

Though initially during 2003, he tried to store the runoff water in the deep and wide gully by providing bori bandhan (sack dam) across the gully with a view to enhance the groundwater recharge and thereby rejuvenating the open well. However, due to high runoff volume and velocity, the sack dam broke away within 10 days of monsoon arrival in the very first year of its provision. It is worth to mention here that bori banchan is a temporary structure and suitable only for handing runoff in very small gully and lasts only for one season. Since, the site was not suitable, the temporary structure could not serve the purpose of reclaiming gully and storing and arresting runoff water during monsoon season.

Then he contacted the local Panchayat Sarpanch Mrs. Laxmi Vishnu Malviya and watershed team and got constructed cemented stop dams in series in this deep gully during 2015 with one at nearby his open well. In all three stop dams were provided in this 1500 m long gully. He immediately further enhance the effectiveness of the stop dams constructed nearby his field by excavating the sunken ponds in his 500 m gullied portion by investing 1 lakh from his own side during the month of March-April 2015. The excavated soil was utilized and spread in the fields for the proper leveling and reclaiming the washes developed in his fields making it more suitable for cultivation. The results of developing sunken ponds not only immediately reflected in the form of enhanced groundwater recharge to his open well, tubewells but other farmers also found the increased water availability from their tubewells. In the very first year of construction of stop dams and development of sunken ponds, Mr. Lokendra Rajput could harvest a good production of onion and potato from his fields. But even then, he was not satisfied by the quantity of irrigation water available from his various sources for the cultivation of successful *rabi* crops.

During 2015-2018, he attended various training programmes organized by ATMA, AICRP on Dryland Agriculture Indore and State Department of Farmer Welfare and Agricultural Development and Department of Horticulture and got exposure to natural resource management activities particularly rainwater management practices being adopted at College of Agriculture, Indore and in

Traditional percolation tank near ridgeline
HARSOLA 2018
7.9.2018

Modified elevated tank construction near ridgeline
HARSOLA 2018
Elevated tank - Alternate land use of degraded land
7.9.2018

Modified tank construction near ridgeline
HARSOLA 2018
Alternate land use of degraded land
7.9.2018

Elevated water storage tank ready for lining
HARSOLA 2018
20.6.2018
Elevated water storage tank
HARSOLA 2018
20.6.2018
Elevated water storage tank
HARSOLA 2018
20.6.2018
Elevated water storage tank
HARSOLA 2018
20.6.2018

Modified elevated tank construction near ridgeline
HARSOLA 2018
7.9.2018

Modified elevated tank construction near ridgeline
HARSOLA 2018
7.9.2018

Lined water harvesting tank
INDORE 2018
25.6.2018
Percolation tank
INDORE 2018
13.7.2018
Ishwar Singh tank
NINGNOTI 2018
25.6.2018
Percolation tank
INDORE 2018
12.7.2018

Stop dam in the gully through watershed development fund
HARSOLA 2018
20.6.2018
Stop dam, sunken pond and open well location from tank
HARSOLA 2018
20.6.2018
Sunken pond creation in gully for ground water recharge
HARSOLA 2018
20.6.2018
Stop dam and sunken pond arrested runoff immedietely
HARSOLA 2018
22.6.2018

Crop diversification due to enhanced water availability
HARSOLA 2018
7.9.2018

Crop diversification due to enhanced water availability
HARSOLA 2018
7.9.2018

Crop diversification due to enhanced water availability
HARSOLA 2018
7.9.2018

Crop diversification due to enhanced water availability
HARSOLA 2018
7.9.2018

the farmer's fields through operational research activities. During 2017, he came in contact with Dr. P.G. Nadkarni, retired professor from College of Agriculture, Indore and on his suggestions; he visited the Kisan mela organized at College of Agriculture, Indore and at Pune. Since it was not possible to construct a water harvesting tank and storing runoff water even for few days due to high seepage rate of sub soil of the fields, from these exposure visits and persuasion, he got motivated and decided to invest some fund from his own side for the development of a huge elevated lined water storage tank.

For this purpose, he engaged a contractor and got constructed a huge elevated water storage tank in January 2018 by utilizing 3500 sq.m. land and by spending 6.50 lakh. The size of the tank is 57 m x 45 m at top and 44 m x 33 m at bottom with a depth of 7 m. The depth of the tank below the actual land surface is 3.3 m (created through excavation) and above the surface is 3.6 m (created through forming of side bunds with proper side slopes all around). The tank is lined with 500 micron HDPE sheet with proper anchoring on all sides of tank. Since it is provided with side bunds all around, the tank will not be arresting runoff water. The tank is constructed in such a way that it would only collect the pumped water and only rainwater falling over it. The estimated storage capacity of this tank is 14623 cu.m. For the safety and to avoid the accident, the tank area is fenced from all around with chainlink.

Immediately in the month of January 2018, he started collecting the pumped water from the tubewells which were providing groundwater interruptedly at reduced discharge rates. The same has been a regular trend in the various farmer's fields even where excavated water harvesting tanks and sunken ponds are constructed in the lower most portions of the fields firstly to be filled with runoff water and after its use for irrigation using horizontal submersible pump and then with tubewell water for refilling for its further and subsequent uses. Thus conjunctive use of rainwater/runoff and groundwater is ensured by the farmers with water harvesting tanks in Malwa region. Mr. Lokendra Rajput filled the storage tank to the brim. Instead of providing a horizontal submersible pump in the storage tank for irrigating the nearby fields, a unique and innovative approach is adopted by him. He is using the almost defunct open well as sump well and made arrangement of siphoning the stored water from the lined storage tank into open well and then using it by submersible horizontal pump. The siphon pipe is provided with a valve at the open well end so that the siphoning can be easily started whenever required. The underground pipelines are also installed all around the cultivated fields with proper openings and provision of valves for regulating and diverting the irrigation water to different land portions. The provision of underground pipe lines enhanced the water conveyance efficiency and also saved time and labour for proper irrigation. The stored water was then utilized for timely irrigating the onion crop in 1 ha and to potato crop in 7 ha area and he could harvest the bumper crops with this additional irrigation water. After the harvest of the crops, the cultivated fields are planted with various horticultural crops like guava, mango, ber, cauliflower and various vegetables in sequence. Despite continuous irrigation from the tank, the tank still has sufficient water even for providing supplemental irrigation during probable prolonged dry spell in the forthcoming *kharif* season of 2018. Thus, it can be pointed out that within a short period after the construction of water storage tank in his fields, Mr. Lokendra Rajput diversified the traditional cropping system and this is a very encouraging and motivation way of incorporating integrated farming system. Due to availability of sufficient water, 8-10 labours are continuously engaged for carrying out and helping in the farming activities. He is even planning to incorporate a very important livestock component like fish rearing. However, he is reluctant to opt for goat rearing and poultry farming due to social issues.

The excavated soil was later utilized for the reclamation of gullied portion, bringing new area under cultivation by deepening and straightening the serpentine shaped gully and filling the low lying areas. In this way, an approximately 1 ha new area brought under cultivation and this activity stabilized the gully and avoided the chances of further development of gully through checking gully head advancement process. A sizable amount of excavated soil is still piled up nearby and would be used for filling in the lower fields.

The success of Mr. Lokendra Rajput has generated a lot of curiosity among the farmers of the region. In the village Harsola itself, eight farmers have either constructed lined elevated tanks of different sizes by investing from their own or in the process of completion/construction/lining of the elevated tanks. These tanks would be filled with tubewell water and would be utilized during the *kharif* and *rabi* seasons of 2018-19. These elevated tanks are the modified form of earlier traditional storage tanks constructed at the upper most portions of the fields to be filled by open well and then providing irrigation to crops through gravity.

However, Mr. Lokendra Rajput clearly suggested that the rainfed farming system is not adoptable in this region unless special efforts are made to enhance and ensure the water availability at the farm. The development and adoption of integrated farming system also require lot of patience and water management aspect is a key factor for its sustenance. Thus, utilizing all technological and hydrological options available for proper rainwater management and storage of sufficient water either through runoff, groundwater or with conjunctive use of ground and surface, it would be possible to develop an integrated farming system (IFS) with the inclusion of multiple crops and multiple enterprises.

Chapter 6

Water Management Research and Technologies in Malwa Region

In Malwa region, crop productivity suffers mainly due to moisture stress during prolonged dry spells after the sowing of *kharif* crops and mainly towards the termination of monsoon. In this region, the runoff potential is very high and if this excess water is suitability harvested it could be used for irrigating the *Kharif* and *Rabi* crops. The major constraint in growing a second crop with higher productivity in many areas is the lack of suitable irrigation water. The deep ploughing operation not only eradicates deep-rooted weeds but also reduces the bulk density (top 30cm) appreciably and thus increases the moisture retention in the soil profile. This operation results in reduced bulk density and allows the soybean roots to move in deeper layers and also ensures moisture storage in soil profile. The use of mulches and providing vegetative and mechanical barriers at suitable vertical interval also helps in rainwater management and in situ moisture conservation.

The study confirmed that the activity of excavation of farm ponds on the individual farmer's field was extremely useful in turning the mono-cropped area into multi-cropped/crop diversified area and improving the farmer's income and, thus, his/her standard of living. To improve the productivity of the region, the local farmers need technical guidance for proper site selection and designing the tank sizes and suggesting suitable cropping pattern for improving the productivity. Farm ponds in the individual farmer's fields in the Malwa region will play a vital role in irrigation the crops and improving the productivity of these areas. For the construction of water harvesting tanks priority should be given to the gullied portion where tanks can be created with suitable gabion outlet as the initial cost of the tank remains lower than the excavated tank. However, one advantage of excavated tanks over excavated cum embankment tanks is that much more soil is available for spreading in the undulating fields and waste lands making them suitable for cultivation.Thus storing excess rainwater in dugout farm ponds for utilization during the dry spells of monsoon season or for raising a subsequent crop was a promising way to improve the cropping intensity and crop productivities and to stabilize the farming in the Malwa region.

1. Scenario

1.1. Rainfall

The climate of the study area is subtropical monsoon type, characterized by hot and dry summer (except during monsoon season) and mild winters. The Malwa plateau is notable for its cool nights (Shab-e-Malwa) in hot season. The mean annual rainfall of the area is 970.45 mm, most of it is received in the months of June, July August and September. In general August is the wettest month. The winter rains (Mawtha) are generally received between October and January. The mean annual air temperature of the area is 24.11°C. The mean annual winter and summer temperature recorded for last 25 years are 20.65 and 26.51°C, respectively. Thus, the soil moisture regime is "Hyperthermic". The soil moisture control section remains moist for 200 cumulative days whereas it remains dry for 84 days. Therefore, soil moisture regime is "Ustic". The climatic data from Indore reveals that the rainfall covers about 40-50 per çent of the annual PET demand resulting in gross water deficit of 800-1200 mm. The longest growth period (LGP) ranges from 90-150 days per annum. The areas in Malwa plateau that has little soil cover are subjected to drought hazard once in three years. The frequent inter spells of doughtiness in the crop growing period lead to crop failure.

1.2. Rainfall-Runoff Relationships

The rainfall data of the year 1971-1982 were analyzed and it was found that three rain fall peaks were common in normal years,*i.e.*, when rainfall ceases by the last week of September. In normal year, the first peak of high rainfall was in the second week of July, next one in second week of August and the third peak was in the last week of September. It has been also observed that during these periods rainfall continues for three or more days, which makes the soil completely saturated with high quantum of runoff and sufficient stored water was available in water harvesting tank to protect the *Kharif* crops during inter dry spells and/or to apply about 8-10 cm of water at the time of sowing *Rabi* crops in normal years. However, when the rainfall ceases earlier that is in 2nd or 3rd week of August, one life saving irrigation could be given to *Kharif* crops. The effect of life saving irrigation to *Kharif* crop was studied and given in Table 6.1.

Table 6.1: Rainfall-Runoff from Medium Black Soil

Year	*Total Rain (mm)*	*Runoff (mm)*	*Runoff (Per cent of Total Rainfall)*
1971	975	523	53.6
1972	539	220	40.8
1973	1889	936	49.5
1974	868	182	20.9
1975	1376	398	28.9

Year	Total Rain (mm)	Runoff (mm)	Runoff (Per cent of Total Rainfall)
1976	1241	524	42.2
1977	1131	417	36.8
1978	985	389	39.5
1979	675	270	40

Rainfall-Runoff from Deep Black Soil

Year	Total Rain (mm)	Runoff (mm)	Runoff (Per cent of Total Rainfall)
1979	675	140	20.7
1980	930	165	17.7
1981	839	92	10.9
1982	612	42	6.8

Based on the long term data on the rainfall and runoff values recorded at the on station trials and ORP fields, following equation has been developed to predict the runoff.

$$Y = 0.415 X_1 + 0.113 X_2 - 6.933 \ (r = 0.82, R = 0.67)$$

Where,

Y = runoff in mm

X_1 = Rainfall on the day of runoff (mm)

X_2 = Rainfall total 5 days preceding to runoff events (mm)

1.3. Agro Ecological Characterization

Two different watersheds namely Pipliyahana (22°42′40″ latitude, 75°53′45″ longitude) and Umariya Khurd (22°39′32″ latitude, 75°57′05″ longitude) were selected in 1999-2000 for the study. The hydro-geomorphic features of different watersheds, where project sites are located are presented in Table 6.2.

Table 6.2: Hydro-geomorphic Features of the Project Area

Sl.No.	Characteristics	Watershed	
		Umariya Khurd	Pipliyahana
1	Area of the watershed (ha)	193.25	168.75
1.a	Area under mountain (ha)	10.50	0.00
1.b	Area under cultivated field (ha)	167.75	67.84
1.c	Area under uncultivated field (ha)	15.00	100.91
2.	Shape of watershed	Fan	Fan
3.	Shape index	2.07	1.92
4.	Maximum relief (m)	118.10	5.50
5.	Land slope (per cent)	4.66	0.85

Sl.No.	Characteristics	Watershed	
		Umariya Khurd	Pipliyahana
6.	Drainage density (km/km^2)	2.48	1.59
7.	Drainage pattern	Medium drainage texture	Coarse drainage texture
8.	Length of gully (m)	2000.00	1800.00
9.	a) Maximum depth of gully (m)	2.75	1.80
	b) Minimum depth of gully (m)	2.00	1.00
10.	Time of concentration (Minutes)	20.15	58.00
11.	Peak rate of runoff (Cumec)	26.00	18.00
12.	Forest cover (per cent)	5.00	Nil
13.	Canopy cover in forest (per cent)	3.00	Nil
14.	Vegetative cover over mountain (per cent)*	5.00	Nil

1.4. Lysimetric Studies of Water Requirement of different Crops

Consumptive use studies of evapo-transpiration by different crops were made using floating type lysimeters during 1971-77. A gradual increase in evapo-transpiration starting from planting to maturity stage was observed and the maximum value was observed during flowering to fruiting stage. Residual moisture left after the harvest of *Kharif* crops was found to be 200 to 280 mm. This moisture was quite sufficient to raise second sequential *Rabi* crops,*i.e.,* safflower.

Table 6.3: Consumptive Use of Water by different Crops under Rainfed Condition (Mean values) from 1971 to 1977)

Particulars	Crops					
	Sorghum	Maize	Soybean	Wheat	Gram	Safflower
Consumptive use of water mm.	400–500	350–400	400–450	225–250	225–250	200–230

2. Research Achievements and Technologies Developed

2.1. *In-situ* Moisture Conservation

2.1.1. Watershed Development Programme: An Experience in Black Clay Soil Region (1989-1993)

The ORP at Hingonia-Pipliyatapha (76°4′ E and 22° 7′ N) is located in N-W of Indore (549 MSL). This project is in operation since 1986 in the said villages in the lower reaches of river Gambhir. This area typically represents soil, climate and socio-economic condition of Malwa region. The mean annual rainfall is about 980 mm. The soils of the area are typical Vertisols synthesized from basaltic parent material. The soils though fertile and rich in $CaCO_3$ nodules are vulnerable to runoff and erosion as per LCC belongs to II, III, IV and V. Uninterrupted slopes of the large field develop erodible velocities of runoff, resulting in severe splash, sheet, rill and gully erosion. The dry spell in the flowering, dough stages of *kharif* adversely affect the yields even though the total rainfall is quite high.

An integrated watershed management plan for soil conservation works was made in 1989 after a detailed topographical, soil and socio-economical surveys of the area during the year 1987-1988. This plan involved construction details of bunding, various engineering measures and strategy to develop other resources. As a result of these measures, runoff has been controlled and diverted safely. The waterways were stabilized and gully head advancement phenomenon has been controlled. The silt is being trapped in the field along-with bunds, waste weirs, loose boulder and gabion structures and diversion drains.Field bunding has been done in an area of about 250 hectare. Considering the soil type, topographical and climatic conditions, 1.0 sq.m. cross-section of 0.75 m high bunds has been constructed. Minor levelling has also been carried out in few locations. In all, 33 waste weirs, 8 loose boulder structures and 3 gabion structures have been constructed at suitable sites. Waterways of about 1800 m have been provided in the area for safe disposal of excess water. Two water-harvesting tanks have been constructed in the area to collect the excess runoff from the large chunk of the watershed. The storage capacities of the tanks are 10,000 cu.m and 17,000 cu.m. with the catchment area of 50 hectare and 55 hectare, respectively.The earlier cropping systems were substituted by soybean + arhar, soybean-wheat, soybean-linseed, soybean-chickpea and soybean-safflower. A complete package of conservation agronomic practices with improved/high yielding varieties, fertility and plant protection management techniques for different crops have been demonstrated in the watershed.

Data collected from 1993 to 1996 on daily rainfall and groundwater level in the wells were analyzed. All the wells exhibit the natural phenomenon of water level variations. Water level in wells starts receding after the monsoon and reaches to lowest level just before the monsoon. During the monsoon, water level rises due to well recharge. The difference between maximum and minimum depth of water level in wells recorded just before the monsoon and after monsoon, respectively. This difference reflects the total rise in groundwater as a result of recharge. In cases when water table goes down even below the bottom of wells, rise in groundwater table was calculated considering maximum water table depth at bottom of well. Close look of data reveals that even in the year of scanty rainfall, water remains available in most of the wells throughout the year.

Regression analysis was carried out to find correlation between rainfall and rise in water table due to recharge. Analysis indicates that annual rainfall and annual rise in water table are highly correlated (R^2 = 0.9981). Efforts were made to find out correlation between percentage change in comparison to previous year values of rainfall and rise in water levels. It was found that percentage change over the average value are highly correlated (R^2 = 0.9961). Regression equations developed describing the relationships between various factors are given below:

$$W_1 = 0.0151\ (R_1) - 8.036\ (R^2 = 0.9981) \qquad \text{.....................(1)}$$

$$W_2 = 2.0900\ (R_2) - 2.370\ (R^2 = 0.9556) \qquad \text{.....................(2)}$$

$$W_3 = 1.4600\ (R_3) + 6.070\ (R^2 = 0.9961) \qquad \text{.....................(3)}$$

where,

R_1 - Annual rainfall (mm),

W_1 - Average increase in water levels in well (m),

R_2 - Percentage change in rainfall over previous year (per cent),

W_2 - Percentage change in water levels in wells over previous year (per cent),

R_3 - Percentage change in rainfall over average values (per cent), and

W_3 - Percentage change in water level in wells over average value (per cent).

High rainfall year 1994 and 1996 exhibits a wide difference in percentage change in rainfall and rise in water level over previous year values. In 1994, the change in rainfall and rise in water level were 36.04 and 73.52 per cent over previous year values while in 1996, these were 40.66 and 95.70 percent, respectively. This reflects lesser percentage recharge in 1995. This phenomenon can be well understood by close scrutiny of rainfall distribution during the year. Uneven distribution of rainfall contributed very little towards groundwater and more surface runoff in 1995 while in the year 1994 and 1996, more uniform distribution of rainfall resulted higher recharge and rise in water table.

As a result of soil and water conservation programmes, moisture availability in soil profile and water availability in well increased. A significant improvement in water potential was recorded in this area. During pre-project period, the life span of shallow wells used to be only 2-3 months after the cessation of monsoon rains. However, in the post-project era, wells do not dry up till as late as March in the subsequent year. There was increased water availability in the watershed due to impounding and recharging of water. As such, the irrigated area has increased from 28 hectare during 1987-88 to 168 hectare during 1994-95. This increase in irrigation potential in wells due to water recharge resulted an increase in area under *Rabi*. Before project, only 166 hectare was under *Rabi* crops while in 1996-97, it increased to 300 hectares. An increase in area under wheat by 44 percent clearly reflects the impact of programme as increase in water availability in wells. Introduction of new varieties, improved management practices coupled with more available water in wells resulted in increase in land productivity of *Kharif* and *Rabi* crops.

The indirect advantage of the development of water bodies in the watershed can be assessed from the increase in number of animals in the watershed resulting in an appreciable increase in the milk production. The number of buffaloes, cows (Jersi) and goats increased from 88, 2 and 35 in 1987-88 to 260,43 and 120, respectively in 1995-96 mainly due to availability of drinking water (surface as well as groundwater) and fodder.

Table 6.4: Soil and Water Conservation Measures followed in Watershed

Particulars	*nos./m Length/Hectare*
Graded bunding	1500 m
Levelling	8 hectare
Gabion structures	3 nos.
Loose boulder structures	8 nos.
Waste weirs	33 nos.
Water ways	1800 m
Diversion drains	1375 m
Terracing	5 hectare
Spurs	2 nos.
Water harvesting tanks	2 nos.

Table 6.5: Annual Rainfall, Rise in Groundwater and Percentage Change Due to Recharge

Year	*Rainfall (mm) R_1*	*Average Fluctuation in Water Level in Well (m) W_1*	*Percentage Change Over Previous Year (per cent)*		*Percentage Change Over Average Value (per cent)*	
			Rainfall R_2	*Water Level W_2*	*Rainfall R_3*	*Water Level W_3*
1989	624.0	2.30	-	-	-36.15	-66.12
1990	1046.0	4.92	+6.70	+113.05	+7.0	-27.83
1991	779.8	3.70	-25.41	-24.46	-20.2	-45.51
1992	583.7	3.45	-25.10	-6.75	-40.2	-49.18
1993	1062.5	7.82	+82.02	+126.62	+8.7	+15.17
1994	1445.4	13.57	+36.04	+73.52	+47.8	+99.85
1995	946.7	6.29	-34.49	-53.64	-3.1	-7.36
1996	1331.6	12.31	+40.66	+95.70	+36.2	+81.29
Average	977.4	**6.79**	-	-		-

Table 6.6: Monthly Rainfall (mm) in Watershed during Study Period

Month	*1993*	*1994*	*1995*	*1996*
January	0.00	31.00	11.70	9.80
February	0.00	2.80	0.00	0.00
March	0.60	0.00	2.80	2.00
April	0.00	0.00	2.35	1.40
May	6.30	5.50	0.75	9.30
June	134.30	315.40	145.28	54.70
July	394.40	314.80	385.50	676.90
August	277.00	470.40	224.40	269.00
September	201.40	302.60	121.30	227.90

Month	*1993*	*1994*	*1995*	*1996*
October	46.70	2.40	51.50	79.32
November	0.00	0.50	0.00	0.80
December	1.80	0.00	1.20	0.00
Total	1062.50	1445.40	946.78	1331.62
Rainy days	53	53	40	**53**

Table 6.7: Improvement in Water Potential

Particulars	*1987-88*	*1991-92*	*1994-94*
Surface water storage (cum)	nil	27,000	27,000
Dug wells (Nos.)	19	29	29
Shallow/deep wells (Nos.)	3	12	27
Total irrigated area (hectare)	28	77	168
Irrigated area (per cent)	6	17	40

Table 6.8: Cropping Pattern in the Watershed

Crops	*Area (hectare)*	
	Before Project (1987-88)	*After Project (1996-97)*
	Kharif	
Sorghum	48.0 (18.4)	3.5 (1.1)
Maize	4.5 (1.7)	--
Pigeon pea	4.5 (1.7)	7.0 (2.2)
Soybean	132.0 (50.6)	243.0 (78.0)
Mixed crop	9.0 (3.4)	--
Fodder	24.5 (9.4)	40.0 (12.80
Inter cropping	3.0 (1.1)	9.0 (2.8)
Vegetables	7.0 (2.6)	6.0 (1.9)
Miscellaneous	28.0 (10.7)	3.0 (0.9)
Total *kharif*	**260.5 (83.7)**	**311.5 (97.9)**
	Rabi	
Wheat	56.0 (33.7)	233.5 (77.8)
Gram	77.0 (46.3)	33.0 (11.0)
Fodder	1.5 (0.6)	9.5 (3.1)
Linseed	11.0 (6.6)	4.0 (1.3)
Vegetables	8.0 (4.8)	3.0 (1.0)
Total *rabi*	**166.0 (53.3)**	**300.0 (94.3)**

Figures in parenthesis are per cent to total area.

Table 6.9: Productivity of Major Crops in the Watershed

Crop	*Local Variety*	*Grain Yield (kg/ha)*			*Improved Varieties*	*Grain Yield (kg/ha)*		
		87-88	*93-94*	*96-97*		*87-88*	*93-94*	*96-97*
Sorghum	Vidisha 60-1	680	1430	-	CSH-5 SPV-475	1210	3780	3480
Maize	Satha	390	1250	-	Ganga 5	410	2900	-
Soybean	Kali tuar	320	-	-	JS 71-05 JS 335	480	1940	2048
Wheat rainfed	Pissi	280	-	-	Sujata	560	700	560
Wheat Partially irrigated	Lok -1	-	-	-	Sujata Lok-1	960	2200	2420
Wheat irrigated	Wh 147	-	-	-	WH 147 Raj 1555	2200	4260	4350
Gram rainfed	U 21	320	-	670	U-21	380	1340	670
Gram irrigated	U - 24	470	1130	1340	Annagiri 218	560	1840	1756
Linseed	-	-	-	-	ILS 73-25	-	920	830

Table 6.10: Animal Population in Watershed

Particulars	*No. of Animals*			*Mean Milk Production (l/day)*		
	87-88	*93-94*	*96-97*	*87-88*	*93-94*	*96-97*
Buffaloes	88	240	260	4.8	6.2	6.8
Cows	153	103	92	2.5	3.3	3.4
Cows (Jersy) cross	2	26	43	8.0	10.8	12.8
Goat	35	108	120	-	-	-

2.1.2. Efficacy of Soil and Water Conservation Measures in Black Clayey Soil

In a nine years (1990-98) study conducted at College of Agriculture, Indore, it was observed that soil and water conservation measures either vegetative barriers or mechanical barriers caused significant effect on runoff and soil loss from the cultivated soybean planted on plots of different slopes. The plots experienced the excess water almost in the entire crop growth stages during the study period. The reduction in runoff amount and thus the associated soil loss is attributed to increased time of concentration and reduced velocity. The vegetative barriers also caused significant soil deposition on upstream and downstream. It is estimated that average cumulative soil deposition on upstream is 2.6 cm and 2.8 cm in the plots with 1.5 and 1.0 per cent slope. The respective figures are 0.52 cm and 0.58 cm on downstream, respectively. The moisture content also increased by 1 to 4 per cent on upstream which ensured better crop stand on the lines adjoining to vegetative hedges.

The soil moisture content also increased up to 3 m from the vegetative barriers as grasses utilize moisture for their growth and development. These barriers thus increased moisture availability on upstream by 1 to 4 per cent. The crop yield on upstream side remained higher than the downstream side. This may be attributed to higher moisture content on upstream due to vegetative barriers. Thus from the foregoing discussion, it may be pointed out that the vegetative barriers cause significant soil deposition thereby control the erosion, and increase the water availability to crops.

Based on the experiment conducted for last ten years, it may be concluded that the soil and water conservation measures are effective means of conserving runoff and associated soil loss from the vertisols of Malwa region. At the same time, the vegetative barriers are found as effective as mechanical barriers in controlling the runoff and soil loss and thus they can be a suitable alternative to mechanical bunds or can be grown along them to support and strengthen it.

Table 6.11: Gravimetric Moisture Content (Per cent) at different Time

Date	*Location*	*Check (Slope per cent)*			*Treated (Slope per cent)*	
		2.0	*1.5*	*1.0*	*1.5*	*1.0*
15.9.95	U/S	17.1	17.1	17.2	17.8	17.9
	D/S	16.3	16.1	16.0	16.5	16.3
18.9.95	U/S	18.1	18.3	18.3	18.6	18.8
	D/S	17.8	17.8	18.0	17.9	18.2
22.9.95	U/S	17.8	17.9	17.9	18.1	18.3
	D/S	17.2	17.3	17.3	17.6	17.8
16.10.95	U/S	15.6	15.7	15.8	15.8	15.9
	D/S	13.0	13.3	13.3	13.5	13.6

2.1.3. Effect of Land Reclamation and Tillage Activities for Increasing Productivity - Experiences in Black Soils of Malwa Region

Under dryland agriculture, not only the total amount of rainfall is insufficient but its distribution also fails to synchronise with evapo-transpiration requirement of crops. For this reason, the success of dryland crop depends on the availability of stored soil moisture. Similarly, in dry land agricultural watersheds, most of the rainwater is lost as surface runoff creating drought conditions and serious erosion hazards due to poor management practices. Thus, there is a need for conservation of rainwater in-situ. Tillage practice is one of the measures for retention of rainwater and its conservation in the soil. Deep tillage practice has also been from crop productivity and profitability point of view. It is a well-known fact that due to urbanization, industrialization, development of problematic soils, the per capita land availability is reducing day by day. It is, therefore, required to bring new area under cultivation wasteland development and bringing fallow land into cultivation to meet out the increasing demand of food grains. The area lying barren for the several years should also be brought under utilization by reclamation process. At the same time, efforts should be made to increase the productivity from the existing cultivated fields. Removal or suppression of weeds (either surface or subsurface weeds) would aid to increase the productivity. Though various attempts have been made to suppress the surface weeds through chemicals, almost no activity has been carried out to remove underground lateral roots of the trees grown on the field boundaries which otherwise interfere with the cultivation operations. These lateral roots also develop suckers during the cropping period and reduce the overall productivity of land by becoming competitor of the crop. Thus, bringing new area under cultivation and removal of subsurface weeds will certainly increase the land productivity. Keeping the above very important factors in view, the present study was carried out during 2003, 2004 and 2005-06 in village Barlai and Jaitpura (Dist. Indore) Operational Research project and under ICAR funded adhoc research project on rainwater management.

The soils of these villages are characterized by swell shrink property during wetting and drying. During hot summer months due to high evaporation rate, the cracks of about 5 to 15 cm width and 1 to 2 m deep are formed. In general, the pH range of the soils varies from 7.3 to 8.5, which is almost near normal and suitable for the growth of the most of the crops, vegetables, fruit plants, fuel and timber trees. The organic carbon content varies from 0.25 to 1.00 per cent in surface and 0.10 to 0.75 per cent in the sub surface of soils. Few sites, mainly infested by weeds were identified and deep tillage operations were carried out using crawler drawn MB plough and reversible plough. One suitable site at Barlai was also identified for the construction of excavated tank and heavy earth moving machinery was used for the development of tank.

2.1.4. Bringing New Area Under Cultivation in Village Barlai

In the present case, a suitable site was selected for the construction of a water-harvesting tank utilizing crawler tractor. The excavated soil of the tank area was lifted through tractor trolley and was spread over a fallow undulating area (120m x 6m) in the month of May-June 2003, which was lying unused for the decades due to undulating topography. The same area was brought under cultivation immediately during the *Kharif* season 2003-04. The portion was planted with the soybean + sorghum crop which produced about 10q/ha soybean + 30q/ha sorghum. If the market value of such portion is calculated even at a very conservative rate, it was observed that Rs. 100000 benefits the farmer. Again this new area is planted with gram/wheat during *Rabi* 2003-04 which also fetched a handsome return from the otherwise unused land. Similarly, the planting of soybean in *kharif* 2004-05 and gram in *Rabi* 2005 also yielded good crops and proved to be remunerative to the farmer.

It is, therefore, very clear from the above that wherever possible the unused area should be brought under cultivation even by spreading the excavated soils to such portion. This allows growing a good crop in the unused portion. Similarly, if field boundaries are planted with various agroforestry components, their lateral roots might enter up to 100m into the fields and may interfere with the cultivation operations and thus may reduce the productivity of the field. These roots can be destroyed using deep ploughing machines specifically M.B. plough. Though these are site specific problems and should be tackled selectively to increase the area under cultivation and to increase the land productivity.

In the village Barlai, it was observed that the lateral roots of the trees grown/ planted on the field boundaries entered into the fields' laterally even up to 100 m inside and interfere with the cultivation operations. These lateral roots used to develop suckers during the cropping period and thus became competitor with the crop. This reduced the overall productivity of the land.In the present study during the year 2003-04, such fields in the village Barlai were identified. About 12 ha of such fields were then ploughed using a crawler tractor drawn M.B. Plough which turned the soil up to 45 cm. At this depth, the lateral roots were quite visible and were then destroyed due to deep ploughing operation. The destroyed roots were collected and removed from the fields. The removal of such weeds in large quantity thus allowed production of good crop despite the formation of dead furrows and slight disturbance in the field leveling while operating MB plough. However, chances of field disturbance can be avoided if reversible plough is used while deep ploughing.

Effect of Deep Ploughing in Barlai

During 2005-06 in village Barlai a tank (Pradeep Tank), has been considered for fish rearing studies. During 2005-06, in the adjoining fields to this tank (2.5 ha) deep ploughing operations were carried out using reversible mould board plough. The deep ploughing operation not only eradicated deep-rooted weeds but also reduced the bulk density (top 30cm) appreciably. The data clearly indicated that the tillage operation reduced the bulk density of vertisol and increased the moisture retention in the soil profile. The deep ploughing operation resulted in reduced bulk density and allowed the soybean roots to move in deeper layers. During the monsoon season 2005-06, the deep tillage operation ensured in-situ moisture conservation in these fields as lot of rainwater percolated into the deeper layers. The higher root density and root proliferation in ploughed field also ensured better crop growth and increased productivity. This resulted in 10.1 quintal extra yield of Soybean (var.J.S.-335) from 2.5 ha ploughed fields in comparison to unploughed field. Even at the time of harvest, the ploughed field retained higher soil moisture, which allowed the dry sowing of gram with satisfactory germination without any presowing irrigation.

It is also observed that the fields, which remained unploughed, were required to provide life saving irrigation to Soybean crop (as was the case in village Dakachya). However, no irrigation was provided from this tank to adjoining Soybean crop grown on the fields with deep tillage operation. It is, therefore, apparent that deep tillage has resulted in higher root length density, soil moisture content and reduced bulk density. The better soil-water and plant relationship has enhanced crop growth and overall productivity of soybean when grown in *Vertisols*. The deep tillage also ensured better residual moisture even after the harvest of soybean without causing any appreciable cracks.

Similarly, during the *rabi* season 2005-06, the deep tillage operation ensured sufficient residual moisture in the fields after the harvest of Soybean crop and allowed dry sowing of *rabi* crop. Therefore, in this case no pre-sowing irrigation was provided and dry sowing of *rabi* crop (bold seeded gram) was carried out. The residual moisture condition ensured the satisfactory germination of gram. Therefore, only one irrigation was provided during the *rabi* cropping season using sprinkler as well as flood irrigation. Flood irrigation was provided in 2.5 ha area and 0.75 ha was irrigated using sprinkler. The average yield from recorded from these areas is 16 q/ha and 17.5 q/ha, respectively.Thus due to reduced water requirement, only part of stored water in the tank was utilized for irrigating the adjoining fields. Irrigation from the remaining stored water ensured survival and satisfactory growth of fingerlings.

Therefore, it is observed only because of deep tillage operation which permitted in-situ moisture conservation during rainy season, the water requirement of *kharif* and *rabi* crop is reduced and appreciable amount of water could be retained in the water harvesting tanks for proper fish rearing. On the other hand, in other water harvesting tanks (Manohar, Abhyankar constructed at Dakachya), no water could be retained as all the water was utilized for pre-sowing irrigation required to cultivable *rabi* (Gram) crops. Therefore, the fingerlings put in these tanks during the month of September 2005 could not survive.

2.1.5. Effect of Tillage on the Development of Weeds and Crop Yields in Village Jaitpura

During the year 2004-06, to evaluate the effect of deep tillage on *in-situ* moisture conservation and improvement in the physico-chemical properties of the soil and further reduction in weed infestation, a study was carried out. During *Rabi* season (2004-05) since there was no crop in the fields due to poor rainfall and no limited moisture after the harvest of soybean, the deep tillage through crawler tractor drawn MB plough was carried out in the month of January 2005. At one site, the deep tillage operations helped in removing the weeds mainly *Saccharum spontaneum* which is a dangerous weed. At this site, no crop could be taken up due to severe infestation of the *Saccharum spontaneum*. At the same, this plot resulted in very poor yield of soybean in *Kharif* season. The deep tillage operations could remove about 10 tonnes of root biomass of weed as against only 1 tonne and 100kg from tractor drawn MB plough and cultivator, respectively. In this study, the performance evaluation of deep tillage and farmers practice was made. Two plots of about 0.8 ha and 0.2 ha, respectively were made cultivable due to deep tillage which could be brought under new cultivation in the following *Rabi* season.

During the monsoon season 2005-06, soybean was planted. The deep tillage operation ensured in-situ moisture conservation in these fields as lot of rainwater percolated into the deeper layers. The higher root density and root proliferation in ploughed field also ensured better crop growth and increased productivity. This resulted in increased yield (4q/ha) of Soybean (var.J.S.-335) from ploughed fields in comparison to un-ploughed field. Even at the time of harvest, the ploughed field retained higher soil moisture, which allowed the dry sowing of gram with satisfactory germination without any pre-sowing irrigation.

It is apparent that deep tillage (ploughing up to 45 cm depth with reversible plough) has resulted in higher root length density, soil moisture content and reduced bulk density. The better soil –water and plant relationship has enhanced crop growth and overall productivity of soybean when grown in Vertisols. Thus, tillage is one dimension that changes the physico-chemical properties of the soil that influences its water storage.

2.1.6. Studies on some Low Cost Soil Water Conservation Measures

During 1999 – 2002, loose boulder structures were made to check the velocity of flowing water up to limited extent, but negligible effect was observed in terms of sediment control. Wire mesh net bond boulder structure (rock fill type sand) about 10-15 cm silt deposition in upstream during 2001 and 5-3 cm silt deposition were observed in the upstream side adjacent to the bund during 2001–02. No water storage was visualized. The water stored in the tank was mainly used for cattle in the area and increase in the water table of treated area to about 3 – 4 m higher than untreated area in the month of November. The average value of sediment of loose boulder structures is 0.40 t/ha.

2.1.7. On Farm Studies on the Impact of Conservation Measures on Ground and Surface Water Resources in Rignodia Micro-watershed

During(2001-2007) water leakage in the wells was observed in the treated and untreated areas. It was found that water levels had started receding after the monsoon and it reached at the lowest level before the monsoon. Water level rises due to soil and water conservation measures where the moisture availability in soil profile and water availability in wells had increased. The optimization of surface and groundwater recharge techniques were useful to increase the water availability during long dry spell (during monsoon periods) and thus, stored water can be used during lean period to set maximum benefit by providing life saving irrigation which also resulted in increase in cropped area and yield during the year 2006-07.

Table 6.12: Impact of Watershed Development Technology on Productivity of Important Crops grown at Ringnodia Micro-watershed Based on Sample Survey (2006–07)

Land-holder's Category	*Base Year 1998 – 99 (t/ha.)*				*Surveyed Year 2006 – 07 (t/ha.)*			
	Soybean	*Wheat*	*Chickpea*	*Potato*	*Soybean*	*Wheat*	*Chickpea*	*Potato*
Small	0.70	1.06	0.50	15.54	1.6	3.4	1.4	-
Medium	0.75	2.40	0.60	16.10	1.3	3.9	1.4	12.0
Large	0.80	2.30	0.60	13.00	1.4	3.2	1.0	-

2.1.8. Biological and Mechanical Barriers for Erosion Control

Cymbopogon martini grass used as vegetative barrier planted in paired rows supported by narrow barred graded bund laid out at 0.5 m vertical interval and 0.2 to

0.3 per cent grade and 1 per cent slope; vegetative barrier helped in reducing run off, soil loss and nutrients losses and increases recharging of groundwater during 2001 to 2009. The data (Tables 6.13 and 6.14) revealed that the highest yield of 2031 kg/ ha was recorded by treatment T3,*i.e.*, sowing across the slope + Vegetative barrier, followed by, T 4,*i.e.*, sowing across the slope + Mechanical bund (1841 kg/ha) and T 2,*i.e.*, sowing across the slope (1579 kg/ha). The treatment T1,*i.e.*, sowing along the slope exhibited the lowest seed yield of 1539 kg/ha. It was evident from data that the amount of runoff (mm) and soil loss (t/ha) was highest in T1,*i.e.*, sowing along the slope (69.70 mm; 2.00 t/ha) and the lowest in T3,*i.e.*, sowing across the slope+ vegetative barrier (22.14mm, o.51 t/ha). *Cymbopogan martini* found suitable as a vegetative barrier grown along the bund to strengthen the bund and to reduce runoff as well as soil loss.

Table 6.13: Effect of different Treatments on Soybean Yield (kg/ha) during 2002-2009

Treatments	*Yield (kg/ha)*							
	02-03	*03-04*	*04-05*	*05-06*	*06-07*	*07-08*	*08-09*	*Mean*
T1. Sowing along the slope	1080	1520	1323	1480	1072	2300	1637	1539
T2. Sowing across the slope	1230	1680	1459	1520	1206	2683	1725	1579
T3. Sowing across the slope + Vegetative barrier	1550	1920	1725	2080	1367	3367	2211	2031
T4. Sowing across the slope + Mechanical bund	1200	1840	1511	1620	1273	2767	1841	1841

2.1.9. Effect of Soil Mulch on the Productivity of Crops grown in Vertisols under Rainfed Conditions

It is well established fact that dry matter and grain production is directly related to water transpired by the crop. The success of dryland crops depends upon the water stored in the potential root zone. To achieve high soil water storage, it is essential to plug the pathways of water loss from soil. Various means were found useful for this purpose, the spreading or maintaining of crop residue at the soil surface as mulch appeared promising and economically feasible. It has been reported that immediately after wetting, water loss from mulched soil is lower than that from bared soil, but as the drying precedes the trend reverses and the benefits of residue mulching starts declining. With this background an experiment has been conducted with the objective to evaluate the performance of different types of mulching on the crop productivity, water conservation and their economic feasibility in soybean based cropping system under rainfed conditions of *Vertisols*.

It is evident from the data on seed yield of soybean and safflower that mulch treatments gave significantly higher yield of crops as compared to No mulch treatment except in 2006 where soybean yield was *at par* in all the treatments. In 2006, the continuous rains during the crop growth period seem to be a reason for non significant differences in soybean seed yield. But the soil moisture content was higher at the planting time of *Rabi* crop in the mulch treatments which resulted in better germination of safflower crop (Table 6.15).

Table 6.14: Effect of different Treatments on Runoff (mm) and Soil Losses (t/ha)

Tr.	*2002-03*		*03-04*		*04-05*		*05-06*		*06-07*		*07-08*		*08-09*		*Mean*	
	Run Off	*Soil Loss*	*Run Off*	*Soil Loss*	*Run Off*	*Soil Loss*	*Run Off*	*Soil Loss*	*Run Off*	*Soil Loss*	*Run Off*	*Soil Loss*	*Run Off*	*Soil Loss*	*Run Off*	*Soil Loss*
T1	28.5	0.80	84.4	1.22	95.8	4.4	132.6	3.09	133.5	4.05	9.0	0.30	4.1	0.15	69.7	2.00
T2	24.3	0.36	57.8	0.59	37.2	1.7	40.0	0.88	102.7	2.40	6.0	0.15	2.5	0.10	38.64	0.88
T3	15.3	0.08	29.2	0.31	32.1	1.2	26.0	0.61	47.0	0.90	3.0	0.50	1.5	0.00	22.14	0.51
T4	19.5	0.15	38.1	0.47	35.0	1.5	32.0	0.68	68.4	1.45	4.0	0.10	0.0	0.00	28.14	0.62

Table 6.15: Effect of Various Mulch Materials on the Productivity of Soybean – Safflower Cropping Sequence

Treatments	*Yield (kg/ha)*		*B:C Ratio (soybean+safflower)*
	Soybean (Av. 3 years)	*Safflower (Av 3 years)*	
No mulching	1605	594	2.20
Glyricidia mulch@ 2 t/ha	1934 (20)	1117 (88)	3.00
Straw mulch @ 4t/ha	1905 (19)	1248 (110)	3.03
Weed biomass mulch @5 t/ha	1972 (23)	1097 (85)	3.02
Soil mulch	1779 (11)	905 (52)	2.63
Polythene mulch	1990 (24)	1142 (92)	2.91

Values given in the parenthesis are the per cent increase over no-mulch treatment.

Table 6.16: Effect of Mulches on the Germination and Soil Moisture Content at the Time of Sowing of Safflower

Treatment	*Germi-nation (Per cent)*	*Per cent increase over Control*	*Av. Soil moisture (per cent Ov) at the Time of Sowing of Safflower*				
			Soil Depth (cm)				
			0-20	*20-40*	*40-60*	*60-80*	*80-100*
No mulching	41	-	21.4	23.2	26.7	27.9	29.9
Glyricidia mulch @2 t/ha	56	37	22.3	24.7	26.9	28.6	29.7
Straw mulch @4 t/ha	64	56	24.7	27.9	30.2	31. 2	32.7
Weed biomass mulch @ 5 t/ha	69	68	24.8	30.3	36.3	37.3	38.1
Soil mulching	49	20	21.6	24.9	34.9	36.7	37.6
Polythene mulch	64	56	31.2	33.9	37.8	38.9	41.5

Overall results suggest that for *in-situ* moisture conservation, mulching with different materials is useful for conserving soil moisture, controlling weeds with enhanced soybean productivity by 11 to 24 per cent as compared to no mulch treatment. The productivity of subsequent *Rabi* crop *i.e.,* safflower due to mulching has increased to the tune of 52-110 per cent. Polythene mulch (ordinary grade), straw mulch, weed biomass mulch and *Glyricidia* green leaves mulch have been found effective in conserving *in-situ* soil moisture and enhancing productivity of soybean–safflower sequence in medium to deep *Vertisols* under dryland conditions. Mulching has been found economically viable (Tables 6.15 and 6.16).

2.1.10 Effect of Land Configuration on the Productivity of Soybean

Madhya Pradesh is endowed with well distributed rains ranging from 700 to 1200 mm. *Vertisols* with good moisture holding capacity can be used to grow short-duration soybean by adopting sound land management practices such as Broad bed and furrow system (BBF), Ridge and furrow system (RF) otherwise about 2.02 m ha accounting for 6.57 per cent of the total area of the state were remain under unsown. The adoption of proper land configuration system will help to increase income to the farmers besides preventing land degradation due to runoff and soil erosion.

The small changes through land configuration in flat field conditions may help in improving the productivity of *Vertisols* of *Malwa* region as at present extensively the flat bed cultivation system is more popular, which faces the problem of water logging and poor aeration thereby affecting crop productivity adversely. Using light machinery like bund former and *Desi Hal* with minor modification may improve the physical conditions and drain ability. It is assumed that land treatments will help to improve soil physical conditions, root development and overall productivity in *Vertisols*. Reduction in seed size is resulting in over plant population therefore, reduced seed rate may help in maintaining optimum plant population with this hypothesis a comparative study with 100 per cent seed rate and reduced seed rate was carried out.

The study revealed that there was a significant effect of land configuration treatments on the seed yield. It was highest in T2: BBF-45 cm (2347 kg ha^{-1}), followed by T3: RFS-45cm (2238 kg/ha), T4: RFS-60 cm (2157 kg/ha). All these three treatments were found statistically *at par* but significantly superior to T1: FBS-45cm (1780 kg/ha).

Among seed rates the highest seed yield was recorded in case of S_2: 60 kg/ ha (2327 kg/ha), followed by S_1: 80 kg/ha (2162 kg/ha) and lowest in S_3: 40 kg/ ha (1902 kg/ha). Treatments *viz.*, S_2 and S_1 were statistically *at par* but statistically superior to S_3. Interactive effect of land configuration and seed rate was also found significant being highest seed yield recorded by T3S_2 *i.e.*, RFS-45cm + seed rate of 60 kg/ha (2657 kg/ha) and the lowest by T1S_3 *i.e.*, FBS-45 cm + seed rate of 40 kg/ha (1657 kg/ha).

The higher root length was recorded in the treatments T2S1, T3S1 and T4S1 as compared to T1S1 that is flat bed planting. The per cent increase in the root length due to land configuration treatments was more than 50 per cent. The maximum root length was observed in T3S1 *i.e.*, RFS-45cm + seed rate of 80 kg/ha (61 per cent more), followed by, T2S_1 *i.e.*, BBF-45 cm + seed rate of 80 kg/ha (57 per cent more), T3S_1 *i.e.*, RFS-45cm + seed rate of 80 kg/ha (50 per cent more) as compared to T1S_1 *i.e.*, FBS-45cm + seed rate of 80 kg/ha, which exhibited minimum root length of 28 m.

2.2. *Ex-situ* Water Harvesting

2.2.1. Farm Pond Designs and Dimensions

Types of Farm Ponds

As per the method of construction and their suitability for different topographic conditions, farm ponds could be classified into three categories *viz.*:

i. Excavated ponds suited for flat topography
ii. Excavated cum embankment type ponds.

For black soil regions with mild to moderate sloping topography, excavated ponds are better suited, Excavated farm ponds are of three types according to their shape. They are:

i. Square,
ii. Rectangular, and
iii. Circular ponds.

Among these, the circular ponds have the geometrical advantage that they have the highest storage capacity and least perimeter for a given surface area and side slopes. However, their curved shape is a disadvantage in construction. Hence, either square or rectangular ponds are suggested.

Design of Farm Pond

Survey of the catchment gives knowledge of the extent of the contributing catchment and other catchment characteristics that are vital for successful planning of the pond size. In undulated areas and areas with defined topography, delineation of the catchment boundary is not a difficult task. However, when the topography is relatively flat, as in case of black soils, contouring of the area may become necessary to demarcate the contributing catchment. For this purpose, grid of either 15 or 30 m may be followed. The grids are to be extended well beyond the tentative boundary from a reconnaissance survey of the area. A contour map with a contour interval of either 0.3 or 0.5 m is prepared for demarcation of catchment boundary. The area can be measured with a planimeter or by means of graphical methods. In case of a bunded catchment, the boundaries are artificially fixed by the main and side bunds. Hence, in such cases the reconnaissance would clearly indicate the catchment contributing to the proposed pond site. This can be easily accomplished by moving in the area and the area contributing can there after be decided by running a closed traverse with a prismatic compass around the boundary.

Survey of the pond site involves the determination of the exact location of the pond with reference to the water course, the positions of the inlet and outlet to the pond, the location of the silt trap and demarcating the area around the pond where the spoil (excavated earth) obtained from the excavation will be stacked. Spot levels on the four corners of the proposed pond and a few additional points, using a dumpy level will be necessary to determine the earth work involved in the digging of the first segment of the pond by the stepping method of construction.

Determination of Storage Capacity

The capacity of the pond depends on the purpose for which the pond is created, the annual water yield, storage losses and the siltation rates. The pond should be of sufficient capacity to meet fully the purpose for which it is constructed. If the pond is for supplemental irrigation, the extent of area to be irrigated, the estimated soil moisture deficiency, which is required to be replenished, the storage losses in the pond, the efficiencies of conveyance and application systems have to be considered. The capacity of the pond also depends upon the catchment size and factors affecting its water yield. The water yield from the catchment is a product of the interaction effects of the rainfall factors and the physiographic features of the catchment. While rainfall amount, intensity, events of runoff and antecedent precipitation are the climatic factors to be considered; soil topography, land use and surface detention measures such as bunding intensity, *etc.* are the physiographic factors, which influence the water yield. Sometimes it may not be possible for the technical personnel involved to collect all the aforesaid information. Hence, alternatively a reasonable estimate of the water yield can be arrived at by taking the information on annual runoff percent available from a representative research station. In Malwa region, 20 per cent of normal rainfall has been considered for runoff yield.

Information on Tanks Constructed under NATP (2003-2005)

Three water-harvesting tanks were created in the farmers' fields during 2003-04 so that the stored water could be utilized for the irrigation of crops during moisture stress period. The participation of the farmers was fully ensured for this and approximately 50 per cent of the cost of tank was bourne by the farmers in terms of kind or labours/use of tractors, trolley and implements like MB plough, leveler *etc.* The land for the development of the tank was donated or sacrificed by the farmers either from the wasteland/unused land or from the part of cultivated fields. Similarly during 2004-05, two more water harvesting tanks were created in the farmers fields in the adjoining villages Dakachya and Baroli so that the stored water could be utilized for the irrigation of crops during moisture stress period and even for recharging the groundwater. In one case, the participation of the farmer was fully ensured for this and approximately 65 per cent of the cost of tank was bourne by the farmer in terms of kind or labours/use of tractors, trolley and implements like MB plough, leveler *etc.*

Table 6.17: Tanks Constructed under ORP, Adhoc and NATP Schemes

Particular	*Deepak Tank*	*Patel Tank*	*Bhura Tank*	*Dakachya Tank*	*Baroli Tank*
Type of the tank	Excavated cum Embankment	Excavated	Excavated cum Embankment	Excavated	Excavated
Outlet	Pipe	Boulder spillway	Pipe	Natural	Pipe
Length of the tank (m)	95	55	90	45	30
Width of the tank (m)	43	40	32	31	30
Max. depth(m)	2.35	2.75	2.75	1.90	2.00
Storage capacity (Cu.m)	3580	2670	2538	2336	900

Table 6.18a: Tanks Constructed under ORP, Adhoc and NATP Schemes

Pond Name	Manohar	Abhyankar	Sandeep	Prasanna
Location	Dakachhya	Dakachhya	Dakachhya	Dakachhya
Year of construction	2005	2005	2005	2005
Use of stored water	Irrigation	Irrigation	Irrigation	Irrigation
Lining type	No lining	No lining	No lining	No lining
Cost of construction	263000	200000	161800	161100
BC ratio	3.1	4.1	2.3	3.5

Table 6.18b: Tanks Constructed under ORP, Adhoc and NATP Schemes

Pond Name	Devendra	Chain singh	Gajendra
Location	Panod	Dakachhya	Panod
Year of construction	2006	2006	2006
Present status	In use	In use	Percolation tank
Pond capacity (cu.m)	6500	2400	4888
Pond size	28 m radius*3.0	59*23*1.9	48*48*2
Side slope	1:1	1:1	1:1
Average filling and amount stored	Full	Full	Full
Use of stored water	Irrigation	Irrigation	Recharging
Lining type	No lining	No lining	No lining

Table 6.18c: Tanks Constructed under ORP, Adhoc and NATP Schemes

Pond Name	Hingonia	Pipliyatapha	Sharma tank	Dixit tank
Location	Hingonia	Pipliyatapha	Baroli	Baroli
Year of construction	1991	1990	1999	2003
Pond capacity (cu.m)	10000	10000	7600	1500
Pond size	Irregular	Irregular	190*40*2	30*30*2
Side slope	1:1	1:1	1:1	1:1
Lining type	No lining	No lining	No lining	No lining

Table 18d: Tanks Constructed under ORP, Adhoc and NATP Schemes

Pond Name	Pradeep	Patel	Chaturbhuj	Bauskar
Location	Barlai	Barlai	Faraspur	Jaitpura
Year of construction	2003	2004	2006	2005
Present status	In use	Percolation tank	In use	In use
Average threshold rainfall (daily rainfall)	30	30	30	30
Pond capacity (cu.m)	3500	3500	4000	2500
Pond size	60*40*2	50*50*1.5	85*54*5	40*40*2

Side slope	1:1	1:1	2:1	1:1
Average filling and amount stored	Full	Full	Full	Full
Use of stored water	Irrigation	Recharging	Irrigation	Irrigation
Lining type	No lining	No lining	No lining	No lining

Silting Pattern of different Tanks Constructed under the Scheme

As per the requirement and approved technical programme for the scheme, various tanks of different types, shapes and sizes were constructed during the study period (2005-2008). Similarly technical guidance was also provided to different farmers for construction of water harvesting tanks in their own fields by utilizing their own resources (including land, labour, material, money and machines). Before the construction of these tanks detailed contour survey, other than detailed soil profile studies were carried out for selecting the sites. After the excavation and construction, the detailed contour survey for each tank was again carried out to assess its storage capacity. The details of these tanks are given in Table 6.18e.

Table 6.18e: Details of Various Tanks Constructed under the Scheme

Sl. No.	*Tank*	*Type of Tank*	*Storage Capacity (cu.m.)*	*Year of Construction*	*Types of Machine Used*	*Name of Village*
1	Sandeep	excavated	3054	2005-06	JCB	Dakachya
2	Abhayankar	excavated	2723	2005-06	Bulldozer and JCB	Dakachya
3	Manohar	excavated cum embankment	7457	2005-06	Bulldozer and JCB	Dakachya
4	Prasanna	excavated	2937	2005-06	JCB	Dakachya
5	Chain Singh	excavated	2396	2006-07	JCB	Dakachya
6	Dharmendra	excavated	4623	2006-07	JCB	Panod
7	Gajendra	excavated	4886	2006-07	JCB	Panod
8	Devendra	excavated	7338	2006-07	JCB	Panod
9	Kailash Patel	excavated	3439	2007-08	JCB	Kamliakhedi

It is clear that four tanks each were constructed during 2005-06 and 2006-07 under the scheme. During 2006-07, three tanks were constructed under the technical guidance of the project team. Similarly even during third year of the scheme (2007-08), one excavated tank at Kamliakhedi (Kailash Patel) was constructed under the scheme. These tanks were allowed to fill with runoff water during following monsoon and stored water was utilized for irrigating the *kharif* and mainly *rabi* crops. After the harvest of *rabi* crops, the storage capacity of each tank was again determined for assessing the silting pattern of these tanks.

Table 6.19: Silt Deposition Pattern in different Tanks during following Monsoon

Sl. No.	Tank	Storage Capacity			Shape	Siltation (cu.m.)	Per cent Siltation
		05- 06	06- 07	07- 08			
1	Sandeep	3054	2650		Rectangular	404	13.23
2	Abhayankar	2723	2646		Rectangular	77	2.82
3	Manohar	7457	7792		Rectangular	-335	- 4.49
4	Prasanna	2937	2740		Rectangular	197	6.71
5	Chain Singh		2396	2002	Rectangular	394	16.44
6	Dharmendra		4623	4406	Circular	217	4.69
7	Gajendra		4886	4425	Rectangular	461	9.44
8	Devendra		7338	6586	Circular	752	10.24

The silt deposition pattern of the tanks indicated that almost all the tanks received silt load along with the runoff water as there was reduction in their storage capacities immediately after the monsoon season or after the utilization of stored water. The minimum silt deposition in Abhyankar tank is mainly due to the fact that while construction of this tank firstly, backhoe loader machine (popularly known as JCB) was used for excavating the soil and then finally dressing of side bunds was carried out by the crawler tractor (bulldozer) which not only compacted the loose soil but also maintained the angle of repose of black soil. Therefore, due to stable and compacted sides, the sliding and then deposition of soil in the tank bed was not observed after the filling and emptying process (rise and fall of water level due its use) in the tank. Similarly, it was also observed that while construction of this tank, the excavated soil was not spread immediately in the adjoining fields but away from the tank site mainly to fill the washes and low lying areas to make the undulating fields leveled as far as possible. Therefore, the loose soil could not be carried away along with the runoff water to be deposited in the tank area. Thus, the minimum silt deposition in this tank was observed. Similarly, in case of Manohar tank, the negative value of the siltation clearly indicated that this tank was deepened after one year of its construction to increase its storage capacity. However, it was revealed that while deepening about 150 trolleys excavated soil was lifted away amounting to increase in the storage capacity by 450 cu.m. Considering this, it can be pointed out that only 115 cu.m. silt might have deposited in the tank during the first year which is only 1.54 per cent. This phenomenon is also indicated that use of bulldozer machine while dressing the side bunds, minimized the collapsing of sides into the tank area, thus, maintaining the original shape of the tank. Similarly, the catchment area also did not contribute much silt deposition as it receives runoff water from leveled fields and non-cultivable area.

On the other hand, the tanks constructed fully utilizing the back hoe loader machines (JCB) recorded the higher silt deposition. This was mainly due to the fact that normally JCB machines used for constructing the excavated tanks cut the soil vertically keeping the sides straight and perpendicular. Similarly, while using JCB machine the excavated loose soil put along the side walls to demarcate the tank area and providing side bunds to the tank. In such a case, dumped soil portion serve as side bunds on the soil surface, the unexcavated soil portion in the actual tank area below it remains vertical. Even if the sides are dressed mechanically to maintain the side slopes (1:1 in black soil or even flatter), the soil remain loose and not much compaction takes place. Therefore, it was observed that in excavated tanks the silt deposition was more due to sliding of side walls and bunds with rise and fall of water level in the tanks. The data on silt deposition in various tanks clearly indicated that maximum silt deposition was in Chain Singh tank. It was observed that besides sliding of side bunds this tank receives runoff water from upper catchment area rather than from the field itself through an earthen channel which also drain excess water from old existing community tank. Thus, the runoff water enters in the tank at higher erosive velocity and brings more soil into the tank area. Similarly the Sandeep tank also receives additional water other than its own catchment through a diverted channel which also allowed more silt than those due to sliding of the bunds.

The close observation of the silt deposition of these tanks also pointed out that the circular tanks in general recorded less silt deposition in to the tank than the rectangular tanks. This is probably due to reduced perimeter (length of side bunds) in the circular tank resulting lesser sliding of soil mass than the rectangular tank of identical storage capacity. The contour maps and 3-D view of all these tanks before and after one season clearly showed the changes in the slopes of side bunds. It is very clear that in all the tanks the side bunds became flatter than the original shape after their filling with runoff water and its utilization for irrigation purposes.

Thus, it can be concluded that in excavated tanks constructed using JCB machines higher silt deposition was observed than the tanks where bulldozer was used for compacting the side bunds while construction. Similarly, the tank where the excavated soil was spread immediately on the nearby upstream fields received higher silt load along with the runoff water. The channelized flow into the tank through earthen channel also resulted in much silt deposition in the tank than the tanks receiving runoff water through natural drainage lines in form of sheet from entire area serving as inlet. Even the circular shaped tanks also recorded lesser silt deposition than the rectangular tanks. However, the construction of rectangular tank is preferred due to its compactness and utilization of a land portion demarcated for tank. On the other hand, the circular shaped tank is not easier to construct but also it leaves few portions of the field unused due to its shape and interferes with the regular shape of the field. The above study also suggested that while construction of tanks using JCB machines, attempts should be made to make the side bunds flatter in accordance with the recommended side slopes and making it as compact as possible.

2.2.2. Storage and Lining Requirements and Materials

At most of the places, no lining material was provided as not appreciable percolation was recorded from any of the above tanks.However, some information gathered from the seepage control studies from the tanks constructed in the DARP field has been given as below:

Vertical Side Bund after Construction 2006.

Inclined Bunds after Monsoon Season 2007.

Farm Tank and Seepage Control for Enhancing Land Productivity in Vertisols

At Indore, about 10-25 per cent of average annual rainfall (960 mm) can be harvested and stored in farm tanks for supplemental irrigation and thus, productivity can be increased considerably. Due to high seepage losses, it is not possible to retain the harvested water in farm ponds for recycling when needed to crops during dry spells. The soil of Indore was characterized by considerable degree of swelling, shrinkage and underlain by highly permeable weathered basalt. Thus, an experiment was planned to identify suitable lining materials that control seepage efficiently, economically viable, practically feasible and high longevity for use in black soils (*Vertisols*).

The reduction in seepage losses for constant head of 1.45 m was almost 100 per cent from plastic film (Silpaulin), followed by LDPE film covered with bricks (86 per cent), Cow dung-straw-soil mixture (82 per cent) and soil-cement mixture (44 per cent) while, it was at par and lowest by Bentonite and check (pond without lining). Similar trend was exhibited for the reduction in seepage losses for constant head of 1.15 m and 1.30 m.

The comparison of cost involved for lining farm ponds by different lining materials (Table 6.20) revealed that the initial cost of installation is high for LDPE film lined pond but it does not requires cleaning and dressing in subsequent years and no weed problem was its added advantage. However, the ponds with other lining materials require cleaning and dressing every year.

Table 6.20: Cost Involved for different Lining Materials of Farm Ponds as per January 1991 at Indore

Particulars	*T1*	*T2*	*T3*	*T4*	*T5*	*T6*
Installation cost (Rs/m)	105	105	210	42	105	-
Total cost (Rs)	1910	1410	4660	2395	1760	1000
Cost (Rs/cu m)	48	35	117	60	44	25
Cost of lining (Rs/m^2)	15	9	54	22	13	-

T1: Soil-Cement (8:1) paste 5 cm thick; T2: Soil-Straw-Cow dung (10:1:1) paste 5 cm thick; T3: Low Density PolyEthylene (LDPE) film 400 gauge covered with bricks; T4: Plastic film (Silpaulin) 120 gsm; T5: Bentonite clay application @ 5kg/m^2; T6: Check (Without lining)

Lining on farm pond by Silpaulin sheet of 60 or 90 or 120 gsm controls seepage losses effectively as compared to water loss of 16 l/m^2/hr in unlined ponds.

Table 6.21: Performance of different Lining Materials in Farm Ponds at Indore

Lining Material	*Weed Infestation*	*Dressing and Cleaning*	*Crack Appearance*	*Recasting of Linings*
Bentonite	Sever	Twice a year	Sever	Required
LDPE	Nil	Not required	Minor cracks in brick cover	Not required
Soil-Straw	Moderate	Once a year	Minor cracks in upper portion	Requires at top portion only
Soil- Cement	Nil	Not required	Nil	Not required

Reduction in seepage rate and storage capacity of a dugout pond – a case study

In a study, it was observed that the seepage rate from a dugout pond was reduced to 7 cm day^{-1} after a span of 12 years from the original seepage rate of 12 cm day^{-1}. This was due to the natural silting in the tank area. However, it was observed that the reduction in storage capacity at higher rate was mainly because of excess siltation due to dismantling of inlet concrete structure.

2.2.3. Lifting Systems and Conveyance

For irrigation purpose, the farmers utilized 5 HP diesel pump or electric pump having discharge rate of 10 lps. Since the rainfall pattern was very erratic during 2005 with only 28 rainy days, it was observed that for pre-sowing irrigation, the depth of irrigation varied from 16 to 21cm. Similarly during 2005, for irrigating one-hectare area, 70-75 pumping hours were required. However during 2006 and 2007, the depth of irrigation water required for pre-sowing irrigation was limited only 10 to 11 cm with only 30-32 pumping hours as the area received good and well-distributed rainfall with 59 and 38 rainy days, respectively. During *Rabi* 2006 and 2007, due to good and well-distributed rainfall condition the groundwater availability was also increased. Thus most of the farmers in the region provided pre-sowing irrigations through tubewells for wheat and gram planting. However, the availability of stored water in the tanks constructed under the scheme encouraged and provided confidence to the farmers to grow even other crops like potato, garlic, brinjal, fenugreek, fodder crops in addition to traditional crops like wheat and gram. Similarly the stored water was also utilized for pre-sowing irrigation during *rabi* as given in the Table 6.22.

Table 6.22: Details of Pre-sowing Irrigation Applied during *Rabi* (2006 and 2007)

Tank	*Manohar*		*Sandeep*		*Abhyankar*		*Prasanna*	
	2006	*2007*	*2006*	*2007*	*2006*	*2007*	*2006*	*2007*
Time of Irrigation	Water was not utilised for pre-sowing irrigation from water harvesting tank during both the years.		Nov.	Oct.	Water was not utilised for pre-sowing irrigation from water harvesting tank	October	November	October
Type of Irrigation			Flood	Flood		Flood+ Sprinkler	Flood	Flood
Amt. of Water used (m^3)			1375	1252		2592	1837	1799
Area Irrigated (ha)			1.25	1.25		3.0	1.75	1.75

Tank	*Chain Singh*	
	2006	*2007*
Time of Irrigation	November	October
Type of Irrigation	Flood Irrigation	Flood
Amt. Of Water used (m^3)	1695	1607
Area Irrigated (ha)	1.50	1.50

2.2.4. Efficient Use of Water through Supplemental Irrigation

Effect of Life Saving Irrigation

Runoff water when recycled as irrigation helps in enhancing the yield of crops' depending on intensity of moisture stress, crop growth stage during dry spells. Under normal weather situations, recycling of runoff ensures double cropping as runoff collected water may be used as pre-sowing irrigation (*Palewa*) for getting good germination and plant stand of the post rainy season crops.

Table 6.23: Effect of Life Saving Irrigation on *kharif* Crop Yield in Deep Black Soils

Crop Varieties	*Av. Yield (kg/ha)*		*Per cent Increase in Yield*
	Without Irrigation	*Life Saving Irrigation (8 cm)*	
Soybean (JS-2)	1577	1554	--
Soybean (Bragg)	1795	2050	14.21
Maize (Gauge 5)	2948	3450	17.03
Sorghum (CSH-5)	2928	2574	`--
Black soybean (JBS-1)	1480	1583	--

Table 6.24: Performance of Sequential Crops (kg/ha.) Raised after Life Saving Irrigation

Crop Variety	*Cropping System*	*Yield (kg/ha)*	
		Kharif	*Rabi*
Soybean (JS-2)	Safflower	1554	1530
	Chickpea	1554	845
Soybean (Bragg)	Safflower	2050	1292
	Chickpea	2050	558
Maize (G- 5)	Safflower	3450	1889
	Chickpea	3450	979

Effect of Supplemental Irrigation during Sabi season (2005-2008)

Most of tanks provided one pre-sowing irrigation to the *Rabi* crops. Since, the pre-sowing irrigation requires maximum irrigation water due to cracking pattern and unsaturated soil profiles (10 to 11.5 cm/ha), the irrigation water from the tanks saved atleast two subsequent irrigations from other sources *viz.* tubewells. However, the requirement of irrigation water for pre-sowing irrigation depends on the distribution, amount and stored soil moisture in the soil profiles. Therefore, it is very clear that the amount of water required per irrigation particularly for pre-sowing depends on the soil moisture profile and thus, the cracking pattern in the vertisols. It is, therefore, really difficult to propose practical size of the dugout ponds particularly in black soil as water requirement or area commanded mainly depends on the water front advancement, which is governed mainly by physical properties of soil and ultimately soil moisture storage.

During *Rabi* 2006-07, due to good and well-distributed rainfall condition, the groundwater availability also increased. Thus, most of the farmers in the region provided pre-sowing irrigation through tubewell for wheat and gram planting. However, the availability of stored water in the tanks constructed under the scheme encouraged and provided confidence to the farmers to grow even other crops like potato, garlic, brinjal, fenugreek, fodder crops in addition to traditional crops like wheat and gram.

3. Enhancing Productivity

3.1. Choice of Crops/Crop Diversification

Crop Diversification in *Kharif*

The major crop of the region is soybean. The farmers grow only soybean in the *kharif* season as the rainfall fulfills its water requirement. Further, it has been reported that due to continuous cultivation of the same crop many problems like pest infestation, non-fruiting are responsible for the reduction in yield levels. Therefore, farmers are being convinced to diversify their cultivation practices. However, due to non-availability of sufficient water, the farmers do not take risk of cultivating other crops, which require frequent irrigation even during rainy season when dry spell occurs. If such a source of water is available, the farmers may even opt for high value crops. The project activity under which one water harvesting tank was constructed in 2005, (farmer could irrigate his crop in 10 ha area during *rabi* season 2005 even in the scanty rainfall year by utilizing the stored water in the tank)), developed such a confidence in a farmer (Manohar Choudhary) that he transplanted cauliflower a high value crop which require assured irrigation during dry spells in 0.62 ha (Table 6.25). Further, he transplanted brinjal in 0.25 ha.Similarly, in the adjoining field of Abhyankar tank, about 0.5 ha was also brought under cauliflower transplanting (Tables 6.26 and 6.27). Even at Barlai, due to construction of tank and availability of assured water throughout the year, fish rearing has been taken up continuously for second year. Thus even in *Kharif*, there are other options with the farmers to grow high value crops if sufficient water is available in the tanks.

Table 6.25: Crop Diversification due to Availability of Water during *Kharif* Season

Tank	*Crops during 2005-06*	*Crops during 2006-07*		*Crops during 2007-08*	
Manohar	Soybean	Soybean	Sorghum	Soybean	Maize
		Vegetables			
Abhyankar	Soybean	Soybean	Vegetable	Soybean	Maize

Table 6.26: Change in *Rabi* Cropping Pattern due to Availability of Water in the Tanks

Farmer/Crop/ Tanks	*Area under cultivation (ha)*							
	Gram		*Wheat*		*Potato*		*Garlic*	
	2005	*2006*	*2005*	*2006*	*2005*	*2006*	*2005*	*2006*
Manohar	5.0	1.0	2.5	5.25	-	1.25	-	0.625
Sandeep	1.0	1.25	-	-	-	-	-	-
Abhyankar	2.5	2.25	-	1.75	-	0.38	-	0.25
Prasanna	1.25	1.5	-	-	-	-	-	0.25
Chain Singh*	-	1.0	-	1.00	-	-	-	-

*Tank constructed only during 2006-07.

Table 6.27: Change in *Rabi* Cropping Pattern due to Availability of Water in the Tanks

Farmer/ Crop/Tanks	*Area under Cultivation (ha)*					
	Maize + Barseem			*Brinjal + Tomato*		
	2005	*2006*	*2007*	*2005*	*2006*	*2007*
Manohar	-	0.5	0.75	-	0.25	0.375
Abhyankar	Grown pegionpea and planted fruit plants on bunds of the tank				0.5	-
Chain Singh	Grown pegionpea on bunds of the tank in first year *i.e.* 2006 itself					

This is to highlight that due to availability of surface water in Abhayankar and Manohar tanks, summer moong and vegetables after the harvest of *rabi* crops, was planted during 2006-07 utilizing the stored water for irrigation purpose.

3.2. Mulching

Use of mulches enhances soybean productivity by 11 (Soil mulch) to 24 (polythene mulch) per cent over control and safflower productivity by 52 (Soil mulch) to 110 (Straw mulch @5 t/ha) per cent cover control *i.e.*, without mulch.

Table 6.28: Effect of different Mulch Materials

Treatment	*Soybean*		*Safflower*		*B:C Ratio (Soybean - Safflower)*
	Yield (t/ha)	*Per cent Increase Over Control*	*Yield (t/ha)*	*Per cent Increase Over Control*	
Farmers practice	1.61	-	0.59	-	2.20
Gliricidia leaves @ 2 t/ha	1.93	20	1.11	88	3.00
Crop residue @ 4 t/ha	1.90	19	1.25	110	3.03
Weeds biomass @ 5 t/ha	1.97	23	1.10	85	3.02
Soil mulch	1.78	11	0.91	52	2.63
Polythene Sheet	1.99	24	1.14	92	2.91

3.3. Soil Amendments

The soybean planted with 25 per cent reduced seed rate on BBF or Ridge and Furrow will enhance yield along with the improved physical property of soil, root development and water use efficiency.

Table 6.29: Effects of Land Configuration and Seed Rate on the Productivity, WUE and B:C Ratio

Treatment	*Yield (t/ha) of Soybean*	*Per cent increase Over Control*	*B:C Ratio*	*WUE (kgha/cm)*
Land configuration				
Control (Flat sowing at 45 cm)	1.13	-	2.19	20.08
BBF (0.45 cm)	1.67	36	2.53	27.55
Ridge-Furrow (0.45 cm)	1.65	34	2.43	27.32
Ridge-Furrow (0.60 cm)	1.63	32	2.29	25.71

4. Adoption and Impacts of Technologies

4.1. Productivity, Profitability and Income

The following Table 6.30 presents the economics of the different irrigated crops. The cost of cultivation for the irrigated crops was calculated on the actual basis, whereas, in case of irrigated soybean only increase in yield due to irrigation was considered for estimation of B:C ratio. Since 2005 was the scanty rainfall year, the *rabi* crops could be grown in the area having stored water in the tank as no groundwater was available. Thus, the *rabi* crop could be harvested successfully due to availability and utilization of stored water. Therefore, it is evident that, during abnormal year of 2005-06 with no *rabi* crop in other areas, the owner of the water harvesting tank constructed under the scheme, in general, benefited tremendously with higher B:C ratio. This ratio varies from 3.40 to 6.118 for gram. Similarly for the wheat, it was 3.101. At the same time, irrigation during dry spell to soybean crop increased the yield almost by 4q/ha and for irrigated soybean, B:C ratio worked out to 3.208 to 13.21 depending on the water utilized. The low B:C ratio for irrigated soybean crop is due to higher cost of irrigation.

As already pointed out, during 2006-07, tank water was utilized in conjunction with tubewell water for irrigating *rabi* crops and the overall yield obtained is given in Table 6.31. However, while calculating the cost benefit ratio, the importance was given to pre-sowing irrigation either from tubewell or tank water and accordingly the reduction or increase in yield due to pre-sowing irrigation is accounted for based on the data generated from the neighboring farmers. Since no irrigation was provided to wheat crop from Abhyankar tank, the yield data are not considered for calculating the B: C ratio. It is very clear that for all the *rabi* crops, higher B:C ratio could be obtained due to irrigation from the stored water. However, for the *rabi* crops, particularly gram, it is evident that more area under cultivation/irrigation, higher is the B:C ratio. However, if farmer uses electric pump, higher B:C ratio could be obtained. Due to non-availability of electricity, the farmers are compelled

Table 6.30: Cost : Benefit Ratio of different Crops and Tanks during 2005-06

Tank	*Crops*	*Yield (kg/ha)*		*Cost of Cultivation (Rs/ha)*	*Irrigation Cost (Rs/ha)*	*Total Cost of Cultivation (Rs/ha*	*Gross Return (Rs/ha)*	*Net Return/ Benefit (Rs/ha)*	*B:C Ratio*
		Grain	*Straw*						
Manohar	Soybean	400	354	-	1811.8	1811.8	5812.4	4000.6	3.208
	Wheat	2400	200	6560	2791.8	9351.8	29000	19648.2	3.101
	Gram	1200	900	7525	1594.9	9119.9	55800	46680.1	6.118
Sandeep	Soybean	600	530	-	1034.5	1034.5	8718	7683.5	8.427
	Gram	800	600	7525	3243.3	10768.3	37200	26431.7	3.455
Prassana	Gram	800	600	7525	3419.9	10944.9	37200	26255.1	3.399
Abhyankar	Soybean	600	531	-	660.1	660.1	8718.6	8058.5	13.21
	Gram	980	700	7525	2065.5	9590.5	45500	35909.5	4.744

*For soybean only increase in yield due to irrigation during dry spell is considered.

Table 6.31: Overall Income Earned by Farmers by using Tank Water during 2006-07

Tank	Crop	Area (ha)	Yield (q/ha)	Cost of Cultivation (Rs/ha)	Irrigation Cost (Rs/ha)	Total Cost of Cultivation (Rs/ha)	Gross Return (Rs/ha)	Net Return (Rs/ha)	B:C Ratio
Manohar	Wheat	5.25	27	6880	3273	10153	24300	14147	2.393
	Gram	1	7.5	6600	1656	8256	26250	17994	3.180
	Garlic	0.625	42	73600	2275	75875	138600	62725	1.827
	Vegetable	0.25	250	20000	3792	23792	87500	63708	3.678
	Maize+ Barseem	0.5	115	6400	2276	8676	23000	14324	2.651
Sandeep	Gram	1.25	20	6600	2560	9160	50000	40840	5.459
Prasanna	Gram	1.5	15	6600	759	7359	37500	30141	5.096
	Garlic	0.25	40	73600	2276	75876	132000	56124	1.740
Abhayankar	Gram	2.25	7	6600	759	7359	17500	10141	2.378
	Garlic	0.25	40	73600	2276	75876	124800	48924	1.645
	Potato	0.38	188	59200	1518	60718	83472	22754	1.375
	Moong	0.25	2	4000	1516	5516	7000	1484	1.269
	Vegetable	0.5	230	20000	3792	23792	80500	56708	3.383
Chain Singh	Gram	1.5	18	6600	2133	8733	45000	36267	5.153

to utilize diesel operated pump which increases the irrigation cost and thus B:C ratio reduces.

Thus, it can be concluded that the provision of tanks provides sufficient water not only during *Kharif* season but also during or before planting of *Rabi* crop. Since, the pre-sowing irrigation requires maximum irrigation water due to cracking pattern and unsaturated soil profiles, the irrigation water from the tanks saves at least two subsequent irrigations from other sources *viz.* tubewells. The availability of stored water in the tanks encourages and provides confidence to the farmers to grow even other crops like potato, garlic, brinjal, fenugreek, fodder crops in addition to traditional crops like wheat and gram.

4.2. Constraints in Technology Adoption

- ☆ Construction of surface water bodies required high initial investment.
- ☆ Investment for *in-situ* moisture conservation measures *viz.,* mulching, land configuration *etc.,* and *ex-situ* moisture conservation measures, like farm ponds and recycling of conserve water *via* drip, sprinkler systems were not economically and practically feasible for resource poor farmers.
- ☆ Low land holding was one of the constraints for low adoption of technologies.

4.3. Technology Transfer in Domain Districts of AICRPDA

- ☆ Construction of surface water bodies on farmers fields under the technical guidance of the scientists of AICRRPDA and ORP.
- ☆ Drip, Sprinkler systems were made available to resource poor farmers at subsidized rate under various State Govt. schemes.
- ☆ Restructuring the aged old tanks, wells was promoted by various State Govt. schemes for betterment of rural area.
- ☆ Heavy machines were made available for deep ploughing during summer under *Haldhar Yojana* of the Govt. of Madhya Pradesh.

5. Researchable Gaps

The most rewarding practices that result in greater efficiency of rainwater use are:

- ☆ Identification of crops and their varieties that requiring less water.
- ☆ Identify crop varieties that fit with the favourable period of moisture availability.
- ☆ based on the probability of rainfall and the moisture storage capacity of different soils Develop a conceptual models indicating the most favourable duration of a crop and variety for a given situation.
- ☆ Improve fertility management and rainwater management for dryland agriculture.
- ☆ Synergistic effect of soil and water management and crop management system.

01/21/2004

12/05/2008

12/05/2008

12/05/2008

BARLAI
USE OF MB PLOUGH

The collected weed
From the cultivated
fields.
Effect of deep
ploughing

2005/01/24

07/10/2005
07/10/2005
Root proliferation and rooting depth as affected by tillage operation

CONSTRUCTION OF WATER HARVESTING TANK IN WASTE LAND (Deepak Tank – 3580 cu.m.)

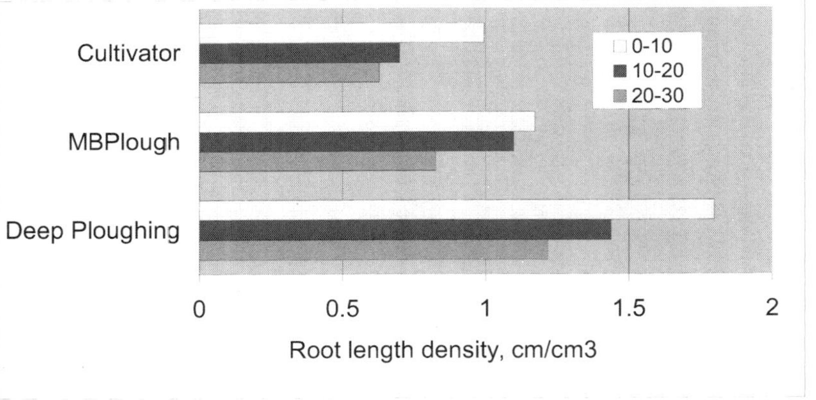

Effect of Tillage on the Root Length Density of Soybean.

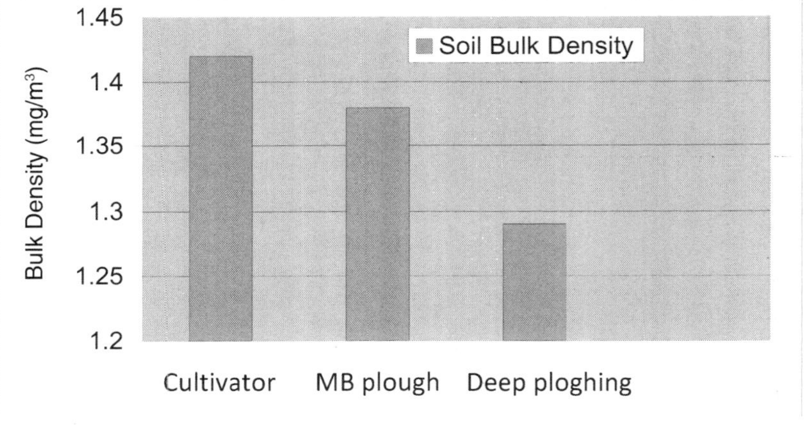

Soil Bulk Density of Surface Layer as Influenced by different Tillage Treatments.

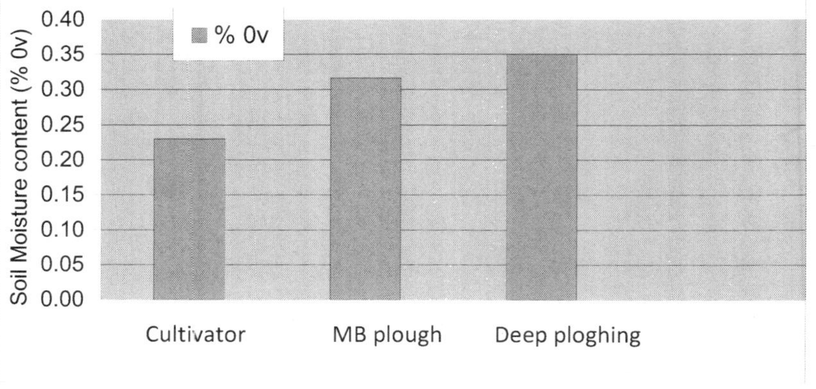

Soil Moisture Content (per cent v) in Surface Soil Layer.

Crop Performance under different Mulches.

Vegetative Barrier of
Cymbopogan martini.

Glyricidia Plant:
Its Foliage Use as Mulch.

Polythene Mulch

Straw Mulch

Soybean Planting Systems for Good RWM.

Broad Bed Furrow

Ridge Planting 60 cm

Raised Bed Planting

Index

S

T

V

W